America's Global Role

Essays and Reviews on National Security, Geopolitics, and War

---

Francis P. Sempa

University Press of America,® Inc.
Lanham · Boulder · New York · Toronto · Plymouth, UK

Copyright © 2009 by
University Press of America,® Inc.
4501 Forbes Boulevard
Suite 200
Lanham, Maryland 20706
UPA Acquisitions Department (301) 459-3366

Estover Road
Plymouth PL6 7PY
United Kingdom

Library of Congress Control Number: 2009928794
ISBN-13: 978-0-7618-4729-8 (clothbound : alk. paper)
ISBN-10: 0-7618-4729-4 (clothbound : alk. paper)
ISBN-13: 978-0-7618-4730-4 (paperback : alk. paper)
ISBN-10: 0-7618-4730-8 (paperback : alk. paper)
eISBN-13: 978-0-7618-4731-1
eISBN-10: 0-7618-4731-6

♾™ The paper used in this publication meets the minimum
requirements of American National Standard for Information
Sciences—Permanence of Paper for Printed Library Materials,
ANSI Z39.48-1992

Contents

Acknowledgments

The following essays and reviews originally appeared in the online journal *American Diplomacy* (www.americandiplomacy.org) : "U.S. National Security Doctrines Historically Viewed," "Trafalgar and the Balance of Power," "Visoionaries of the American Empire: Hamilton and Mahan," "Sea Power and Capitalism," "The War of the World," "The Terrible Shadow of the First World War," "Somewhere in France, Somewhere in Germany," "Inchon and the Course of U.S. Foreign Policy," "Solzhenitsyn: The Most Consequential Writer of the 20th Century," "Ronald Reagan and the Collapse of the Soviet Empire," "Ronald Reagan and the End of the Cold War," "The Sheriff: America's Defense of the New World Order," and "The Asian Eclipse of Europe." I am grateful to the publisher, Michael Cotter, and editor, James Bullington, for granting permission to have this material reprinted in this book.

The following essays and reviews originally appeared in *Strategic Review*, which was published by the United States Strategic Institute and Boston University's Center for International Relations: "Churchill and World War I," "Winston Churchill and the Wilderness Years," "This War Called Peace," "Henry M. Jackson: Hero of the Cold War," "The Grand Chessboard," "Preventive Containment," "Central and Eastern Europe," and "Taiwan and West Berlin." I am grateful to Abigail DuBois, the former managing editor of *Strategic Review*, for granting permission to have the essays and reviews reprinted here.

The following reviews originally appeared in *Presidential Studies Quarterly*, the journal published by the Center for the Study of the Presidency and Congress: "Woodrow Wilson and the First World War," "The Immediate Origins of the Second World War," "Allied Strategy and Tactics in the Second World War," and "Arms Races, Arms Control, and the History of the Cold War." I am grateful to the Center for permitting these reviews to be reprinted here.

"The Geopolitics of the American Civil War" originally appeared in the *Washington Times*. I am grateful to Greg Pierce and the *Washington Times* for granting permission to have the essay reprinted in this book.

"James Burnham and the Struggle for the World" originally appeared in the *Human Rights Review* (Volume 4, Number 2, January-March 2003, pp.62-65), a journal published by Springer Science and Business Media. I am grateful Springer Science and Business Media for their kind permission to reprint the review here.

Finally, thanks are owed to my siblings, Msgr. John Sempa, Barbe Sempa, and Cheryl Sempa Radkiewicz, who invariably encouraged me to write about history and foreign policy, and to my wife, Mary Sempa, who critically read most of the essays and reviews, and to whom, for her patience and love, I happily dedicate this book.

Preface

This collection of essays and reviews deals with various aspects of U.S. national security throughout history. This is a subject that I have been interested in since my high school years in the mid-1970s. My father, Frank Sempa, fought in the Second World War (one of the essays in the book is about his wartime experiences), and worked as a reporter and editor for the *Scranton Tribune* for more than forty years. His love of history and politics sparked my interest in those subjects, and that interest was reinforced and expanded by the fine history and political science professors at the University of Scranton, where I spent my undergraduate years in the late 1970s and early 1980s. One of those professors, Bernard Williams, introduced me to classical geopolitical theories, concepts and scholars that have shaped my world view and approach to the study of America's global role.

Although I pursued a career in law as a county, state, and now federal prosecutor, my interest in history and international politics has intensified. Since 1986, I have been writing articles, essays, and book reviews on historical and foreign policy topics for national and international journals. Some are broad, historical pieces that focus on fundamental geopolitical factors that have influenced and continue to influence U.S. national security policy. Others focus on specific events or historical figures. Still others analyze important books and authors that have contributed to the understanding of history, foreign policy, and America's role in the world. In my previous book, *Geopolitics: From the Cold War to the 21st Century* (Transaction Publishers, 2002, 2007), and in lengthy introductions to four other books on U.S. foreign policy, I have analyzed the geopolitical writings of Halford Mackinder, Nicholas Spykman, Alfred Thayer Mahan, James Burnham, and William Bullitt.

The essays and reviews in this book are grouped into four broad categories: National Security in Historical Perspective, World Wars I and II, the Cold War, and the Post-Cold War World. They were written between 1986 and 2009. The Introduction and Conclusion are original to this work. It is my hope that readers will gain from the book an understanding of the historical evolution of U.S. national security interests and policies so that they may better understand America's global role.

Introduction

In July 1776, the United States was a new, self-proclaimed nation located on a sliver of territory along the eastern seaboard of the center of North America. It was governed by a legislative body that had appointed George Washington as the commanding general to organize, equip, and lead an inexperienced army against the mighty empire of Great Britain. Through a combination of skillful diplomacy, military leadership, courage, and good fortune, the United States defeated Great Britain and won its independence. In the 1780s, however, it was a relative pygmy among the world's great powers.

More than 230 years later, the United States is the most powerful economic and military power on the globe. Its interests are global, and its ability to project power to all parts of the globe is unmatched. It is in every sense of the word an "empire." How did this happen? Why did this happen? The essays and reviews in this book, hopefully, provide some insights into the evolution of America's global role.

The United States did not acquire such power and influence by accident. At the founding, our statesmen and leaders deliberately sought to expand the power and influence of the country. Manifest Destiny, whether expressed as an "empire of liberty" or a country from "sea to shining sea," motivated U.S. leaders throughout the late eighteenth century and during all of the nineteenth century.

To achieve our Manifest Destiny, the United States refrained from involvement in great power conflicts and sought to remove European powers from North America (Washington's Farewell Address), worked to prevent future colonization in the Western Hemisphere (the Monroe Doctrine), exploited the rivalry among the European powers to acquire more and more land (the Louisiana Purchase, the Transcontinental Treaty), and used economic, diplomatic, and military power to remove any impediments to further continental expansion (Indian removal policies, the Mexican-American War).

To maintain the larger Union and preserve the achievements of Manifest Destiny, we fought a terrible Civil War, resulting in the deaths of more than 600,000 Americans.

By the late nineteenth century, Manifest Destiny was achieved as the United States consolidated its control of the center of the continent from the Atlantic Ocean to the Pacific Ocean, and from Canada to Mexico. Unlike the great powers of continental Europe, the United States had no peer competitors in North America, or, for that matter, in the Western Hemisphere. Our geopolitical position in relation to the great Eurasian landmass was similar to that of Great Britain's to the European continent. Indeed, it was during this time period when U.S. and British statesmen began to recognize the common interests between the "English-speaking peoples" that fostered the "special relationship" of the twentieth century.

This development coincided with the general "scramble for empire" among the European great powers, and U.S. strategists and statesmen did not want to be left out of the competition for overseas colonies. Once again, war fostered expansion as the U.S. victory in the Spanish-American War resulted in our acquisition of the Philippines, Guam, and Puerto Rico, and greatly enhanced our influence and interest in Cuba and China. A U.S.-assisted coup led to our annexation of Hawaii. A few years later, a U.S.-assisted revolution resulted in the creation of Panama and the eventual U.S. construction and ownership of the Panama Canal which greatly improved our ability to shift naval power and resources from the Atlantic to the Pacific and vice-versa.

The cataclysm of the First World War further enhanced the relative power position of the United States, and the Second World War decisively ended the age of European dominance in global affairs. For the next 45 years, Europe was but one theater of struggle in the larger Cold War between the United States and the Soviet Union. The demise of the Soviet Union in 1989-1991 brought on the current post-Cold War World.

After a decade of uncertainty in the 1990s, the "structure" of the post-Cold War World began to emerge. One part of that structure was a civilizational struggle between a radicalized and growing part of the Islamic world and Western Civilization led by the United States. That struggle, however, was a smaller part of a larger geopolitical shift from Europe to Asia.

The focus of U.S. security policies in the early twenty-first century is Asia. While the U.S. is fighting Islamic *jihadists* in many parts of the globe, the primary effort (Iraq, Afghanistan, Pakistan, Iran) is in Asia, which, along with North Africa, is the central base of Islamic Civilization. Asia also hosts Russia, North Korea, Japan, and the two emerging economic and military great powers, China and India. As Robert D. Kaplan recently pointed out in *Foreign Affairs*, the Indian Ocean region is now the geopolitical pivot of world politics.

America's global role has evolved in the historical context discussed in the essays and reviews in this book. As citizens of this great country, we need to understand the influence of the past on the present, so we may better comprehend and meet the challenges of the future.

CHAPTER I
National Security in Historical Perspective

U.S. National Security Doctrines Historically Viewed

A country's national security policy is determined by many factors, including external threats, geography, political culture, military capabilities, economic needs, elite opinion, popular opinion (in democracies) and its leaders' perceptions of the country's interests. This last factor frequently manifests itself in what has been called a foreign policy or national security "doctrine." A national security doctrine serves as a guide by which leaders conduct the foreign policy of a country. At its most effective, a national security doctrine is the organizing principle that helps statesmen identify and prioritize their country's geopolitical interests.

In our country's 227-year history, we have had eight major national security doctrines: Washington's Farewell Address, the Monroe Doctrine, Manifest Destiny, the Open Door, Off-shore Balancer, Containment, Liberation, and the current doctrine of Preemption. Although throughout our nation's history specific policies toward other nations or regions of the world have been called "doctrines,"[1] in reality those specific policies were part of, and subordinated to, the nation's larger national security doctrines.

A review of those doctrines reveals that while each was formulated and adopted by our leaders in reaction to immediate foreign policy concerns, each doctrine also addressed certain fundamental aspects of U.S. national security that led future statesmen to follow its broad policy objectives and prescriptions. Moreover, each successive national security doctrine built upon the foundations of the preceding doctrines, resulting in a continuity of policy that has served America well.

George Washington's Farewell Address to the nation in 1796 was largely the work of Washington and his former military aide and Secretary of the Treasury, Alexander Hamilton. It was Washington's final contribution to the nation he helped found and led through its war of independence and early years as a vulnerable republic. Its policy prescriptions became so ingrained among America's leaders and the public, that one hundred years later the great proponent of American expansion, Alfred Thayer Mahan, decried its continuing influence over U.S. foreign policy.[2]

The Farewell Address was one of three complementary national security doctrines that guided U.S. foreign policy for nearly a century; the other two were the Monroe Doctrine and Manifest Destiny. Because these doctrines existed simultaneously and reinforced each other during a significant time period in our nation's history, they will be treated here together.

Washington issued his Farewell Address at a time when the United States occupied a sliver of territory on the east central coast of the North American continent and the young republic shared the continent with Great Britain, Spain and the Indian tribes. Washington and Hamilton both recognized that U.S. independence and its immediate future security depended in part upon the continuing rivalry among the great powers of Europe. The Anglo-French struggles that gave birth to the United States continued after the War of Independence. Despite pro-French sentiment in the United States and the 1778 alliance with France, Washington steered a course of neutrality between the two European antagonists. He realized that the young nation was too weak to involve itself in Europe's quarrels, and that the U.S. was more secure when the European great powers were distracted by continental concerns.

It was Washington's experience navigating the ship-of-state through these troubled diplomatic waters that informed the latter part of the Farewell Address. Those who have read *about* the Farewell Address, without actually reading it, often falsely believe that Washington advised against "entangling alliances," which is in fact a later, rather ideological, Jeffersonian phrase. Washington's advice was far more subtle and sophisticated than is popularly imagined.

"[N]othing is more essential," he wrote in response to pro-French and pro-British attitudes that had vexed his administration, "than that permanent inveterate antipathies against particular Nations, and passionate attachments for others, should be excluded; and that in place of them, just and amicable feelings towards all should be cultivated." The nation's "interests," rather than sympathy or resentment, should determine the direction of our foreign policy. Policy towards other nations that was based on sentiment, Washington warned, would result in "facilitating the illusion of ... imaginary common interests, where no real common interest exist."

Washington advocated a policy of "extending our commercial relations" to all foreign nations, but having with those nations "as little political connection as possible." "Europe," he wrote, "has a set of primary interests, which to us have none, or a very remote relation." Europe will be engaged, he continued, "in frequent controversies, the causes of which are essentially foreign to our concerns." We should not, therefore, "implicate ourselves, by artificial ties, in the ordinary vicissitudes of [Europe's] politics, or the ordinary combinations and collisions of [Europe's] friendships or enmities." "Why," he asked rhetorically, "by interweaving our destiny with that of any part of Europe, entangle our peace and prosperity in the toils of European ambition, rivalship, interest, humor, or caprice?"

"It is our true policy," Washington concluded, "to steer clear of *permanent alliances* with any portion of the foreign world..." He recognized, however, that in some situations "temporary alliances" with foreign nations might be necessary to protect our interests.

Geography ("our detached and distant situation"), unity, efficient government and a "respectable defensive posture," Washington believed, would enable the United States to "choose peace or war, as our interest, guided by justice, shall counsel." The national security goal expressed in the Farewell Address was "to gain time [for] our country to settle and mature its yet recent institutions, and to progress without interruption to that degree of strength and consistency, which is necessary to give it...the command of its own fortunes."

Felix Gilbert has written that the Farewell Address "was the first statement, comprehensive and authoritative at the same time, of the principles of American foreign policy," and it "served as a guide to American foreign policy for over a century."[3] Washington's successors as president throughout most of the nineteenth century repeatedly invoked the Farewell Address when discussing the nation's foreign policy. Eugene Rostow, in his masterful study of the history of American national security policy, described the doctrine proposed in the Farewell Address as "active (and armed) neutrality," which was "altogether prudent and realistic for a world in which the United States was first a small and then a medium-sized power living within a state system dominated by the jostle and bustle of the European balance of power..."[4]

The Farewell Address envisioned an expanding United States. Washington warned against "permanent alliances" because he knew that the new nation needed breathing space to strengthen its institutions and grow geographically. In order for the United States to be able to expand on the North American continent and achieve security from European intervention in U.S. affairs, however, the European powers had to leave. When the United States achieved its independence, Britain and Spain still held sizeable territories on the continent. An immediate goal of U.S. foreign policy, therefore, was to prevent the expansion of European territory on the continent, and, ultimately, to remove the Europeans from North America altogether and limit their presence in the entire Western Hemisphere. This was the first step toward two other U.S. national security doctrines: the "Monroe Doctrine" and "Manifest Destiny."

President James Monroe announced the doctrine that bears his name in 1823, at a time when Russia sought to strengthen its hold on the Pacific coast of North America and it seemed likely that reactionary European powers might help Spain regain its New World colonies, which had established their independence during the Napoleonic Wars. President Monroe declared that the United States would "consider any attempt" by European powers "to extend their [political] system to any portion of [the Western] hemisphere as dangerous to our peace and safety." The United States in the 1820s did not have the wherewithal (i.e, a sufficiently strong navy) to independently enforce the Monroe Doctrine. Fortunately for Monroe and his immediate successors, the British Navy, in support of purely selfish British interests, provided *de facto* enforcement of the Monroe Doctrine.

Once the United States attained great power status, it could and did exert its power and influence throughout the Western Hemisphere. In the twentieth century, the Caribbean Sea became an American lake. U.S. military forces frequently intervened south of the border in Mexico and Central America. U.S. presidents invoked the Monroe Doctrine during the Cuban Missile Crisis in the early 1960s, during the submarine dispute at Cienfuegos in the early 1970s, and during the conflicts in El Salvador and Nicaragua in the 1980s. Today, 180 years after it was announced, the Monroe Doctrine remains an important component of U.S. foreign policy.

The Monroe Doctrine nicely complemented and reinforced the Farewell Address and a new and third national security doctrine, Manifest Destiny. The term "Manifest Destiny" was coined by John L. O'Sullivan in 1839 to explain and to justify the westward expansion of the United States. The policy of expansion, however, had been part of United States national security policy since the founding of the country. Diplomacy and war, both in North America and in Europe, combined to effectuate the U.S. policy of continental expansion. First, Jay's Treaty, and later the Treaty of Ghent ending the War of 1812, largely confined British territorial possessions to Canada. Next, the resumption of the Anglo-French war in Europe in the early 1800s made possible the Louisiana Purchase from France, which more than doubled the size of the United States and gave the U.S. full use of the Mississippi River for the exports of Transappalachian farmers. In 1819, the United States gained Florida from Spain under the terms of the Transcontinental Treaty, skillfully negotiated by Secretary of State John Quincy Adams in the wake of General Andrew Jackson's military exploits. The U.S. victory in the Mexican-American War in the 1840s added a huge swath of territory to the American realm, including land that became the states of Texas, California, New Mexico, Arizona, Colorado, Oregon and Washington. In 1867, Alaska was acquired from Russia. During the rest of the nineteenth century, U.S. forces relocated to reservations any Indian tribes that resisted the pursuit of Manifest Destiny. By 1900, the United States had largely fulfilled the geopolitical vision of controlling the middle of the North American continent "from sea to shining sea."

The greatest threat to the pursuit of the Manifest Destiny doctrine came not from abroad, but from within. The American Civil War threatened to permanently divide the United States into two competing powers. A Confederate victory in that war would have stopped Manifest Destiny dead in its tracks. The European great powers understood this, and so did Lincoln. Several times during the war, Great Britain and France hinted at intervening on the side of the Confederacy, and during the war France gave its support to a puppet regime in Mexico led by Archduke Maximillian. But the combination of key Union military victories and skillful diplomacy by the Lincoln administration persuaded the Europeans to remain neutral, and in 1867 France abandoned Maximillian and its hopes for a New World empire. The most important geopolitical consequence of the Union victory in the Civil War was the ability of the United States to continue its policy of continental expansion.

The overriding common goal of these three doctrines was for the United States to attain effective political control of the broad middle of the North American continent, from the Atlantic Ocean to the Pacific Ocean, and from Canada to the Gulf of Mexico. By 1898, when the next U.S. national security doctrine emerged, a nation that began as a sliver of territory on the eastern seaboard of North America had become a continental-sized giant. It was time, wrote the brilliant naval historian, strategist and proponent of American Empire, Alfred Thayer Mahan, for the United States to "look outward," across the seas and oceans and take its rightful place on the world stage.

American sympathy for Spain's rebellious subjects in Cuba and a more aggressive application of the Monroe Doctrine resulted in the Spanish-American War of 1898. The U.S. victory in that war, both in Cuba, but more importantly in the Far East, resulted in the emergence of a new U.S. national security doctrine, the "Open Door." The immediate object of the Open Door was to create a Far Eastern balance of power that would promote and protect U.S. commercial and economic interests in Asia, particularly in China, which at the time was the scene of great power economic and political rivalry. Quite suddenly, in the late 1890s, the United States became a Pacific and Asian power, annexing Hawaii, and acquiring Guam, Wake Island and the Philippines. Mahan had written in 1890 that the United States needed to abandon the spirit of the Farewell Address. The balance of power in Europe and Asia, he argued, affected U.S. national security. This was not a novel insight of Mahan's. American statesmen since the founding of the country had recognized that European rivalries and ambitions could impact American security interests. The Farewell Address, the Monroe Doctrine and Manifest Destiny were all based, in part, on an appreciation of the relationship between U.S. security and the European balance of power.

Mahan, however, understood that in the world of the 1890s and early 1900s, the United States could not rely on a passive, hemispheric defensive posture to protect its expanding interests abroad. The oceans that separated the United States from Europe and Asia were not moats behind which America could hide for its security. Mahan, instead, viewed the oceans as a great highway of "communications" which would either be used by America's enemies to threaten our security or controlled by America to promote and protect its' overseas possessions and interests.

The Open Door policy was, in effect, a doctrine of overseas commercial and political expansion. To be effective, the Open Door required strong U.S. naval power. Mahan's intellectual call to action in this regard was taken up by his friend and admirer, Theodore Roosevelt.

Theodore Roosevelt was among that rare breed of men (Winston Churchill was another) who combined prolific intellectual output with military heroics and distinguished statesmanship. Before becoming President of the United States, Roosevelt had written several books, including a naval history of the War of 1812. He had also served as Assistant Secretary of the Navy prior to, and at the start of, the Spanish-American War. Roosevelt resigned that position to help organize and lead the "Rough Riders" in the ground war in Cuba.

Roosevelt, like Mahan, believed that the United States had to play a larger role on the world stage. To that end, he vigorously pursued the Open Door in Asia, and greatly expanded U.S. naval power. He hosted and presided over the peace negotiations that ended the Russo-Japanese War (for which he was awarded the Nobel Peace Prize), not simply to end a destructive and bloody conflict, but also to maintain the balance of power in East Asia, a region where the U.S. now had important commercial and strategic interests.

He also announced in 1904, in what came to be known as the "Roosevelt Corollary" to the Monroe Doctrine, that the U.S. would intervene in other nations in the Western Hemisphere to correct "chronic" and "flagrant" wrongdoings committed by governments against their own citizens.

In 1907, in a dramatic gesture of U.S. global power, Roosevelt sent the American fleet around the world! He also secured for the United States control of the Central American isthmus and began construction of the Panama Canal, which, when completed, consolidated the United States' dominant role in the Caribbean Sea region, and made it much easier for U.S. naval power to be transferred from the Atlantic to the Pacific, and vice-versa.

Roosevelt, wrote the diplomatic historian Thomas A. Bailey, "understood the role of the United States in the world of power politics more clearly than any of his predecessors and most of his successors." "He did more than any previous President," continued Bailey, "to swing the United States out of its purely continental orbit."[5]

Just as the United States was entering this period of overseas expansion, the European great powers lurched ever so slowly toward the catastrophe of the First World War. In 1871, after three short, successful wars, German Chancellor Otto von Bismarck grouped many states of the former Holy Roman Empire into the German Empire. Suddenly, the center of the continent was occupied by a populous, growing, industrial power. The Concert of Europe that had been crafted by the diplomats at the Congress of Vienna was coming undone.

For the next twenty years, Bismarck pursued a skillful diplomacy that promoted German interests *within* a relatively stable European balance of power. In the early 1890s, however, the new German Kaiser, Wilhelm II, removed Bismarck from office and eagerly launched a naval program that directly threatened British supremacy at sea. Gradually, the great powers of Europe formed alliances and armed themselves at an ever accelerating pace. A new threat to the continental balance of power had emerged, and Great Britain, as before, assumed the role of Offshore Balancer by throwing its weight, to paraphrase Sir Eyre Crowe, on the side opposed to the strongest power or alliance of powers on the continent.

The First World War was the last global conflict in which Britain acted as the principal Offshore Balancer to uphold or restore the European balance of power. Toward the end of that war, the United States emerged as Britain's partner as an Offshore Balancer. The decision of President Wilson and the U.S. Congress to go to war in Europe in 1917 marked the beginning of a new U.S. national security doctrine that lasted until the end of the Second World War. Between 1917 and 1945, the United States became the Offshore Balancer of Europe *and* Asia because its statesmen gradually recognized the potentially lethal threat to U.S. security posed by a hostile power or alliance of powers that gained control of the major power centers of Eurasia.

Mahan, as early as 1900, sensed that the United States was emerging as a geopolitical partner, and eventual successor, to the British Empire. In his books and articles, Mahan noted that Britain had since the sixteenth century supported, anchored, funded then led grand coalitions of lesser powers to defeat successive attempts at European hegemony by the Hapsburgs, Louis XIV's France, and Napoleon's France. In the mid-to-late nineteenth century, Britain acted to restrain Russian expansion in Central Asia, a rivalry that became known as "the great game." In *The Interest of America in International Conditions*,[6] originally written in 1910, Mahan foresaw that the United States would ally itself to Britain, France and Russia to oppose German attempts at continental hegemony. That is precisely what the United States did twice during the next thirty years.

As the name Offshore Balancer implies, the United States during this time period did not continuously participate in the global balance of power. Instead, it intervened only as a last resort; only when it became unmistakably clear that its weight was needed to uphold or restore the balance of power in Europe or Asia. In the First World War, the U.S. entered the conflict three years after it began. Following the war, American forces returned home and the United States refused to participate in newly created collective security arrangements, even when it became apparent in the thirties that Germany threatened to dominate Europe .

In the Second World War, the United States waited to enter the war until Germany had conquered almost all of Europe, and Japan had occupied key parts of China and attacked U.S. possessions in the Pacific. Only after being attacked by the Japanese and a subsequent German declaration of war, did the U.S. intervene in Europe, Asia and Africa on a massive scale to defeat the Axis powers and attempt to restore the balance of power in Europe and East Asia. In so doing, it became the dominant power in both regions and soon focused its attention on maintaining global rather than simply regional balances.

In the larger geopolitical sense, the Second World War did not end the threat to the global balance of power; it merely replaced one potential Eurasian hegemon (Hitler's Germany allied with Imperial Japan) with another (the Soviet Union). The security threat that caused the United States to enter the Second World War still existed after the war. Indeed, Winston Churchill, who did so much to alert America and the rest of the world to the strategic threat posed by Hitler's Germany in the 1930s, wrote after the war that "we find ourselves still confronted with problems and perils not less but far more formidable than those through which we have so narrowly made our way."[7]

When the Second World War ended, it was by no means inevitable that the United States would remain in Europe and Asia. President Franklin Roosevelt had informed Soviet dictator Josef Stalin that U.S. troops would return home within two years after the war's end. FDR, it seems, like Wilson before him, was willing to entrust the world's future security to an international organization, the United Nations. FDR's successor as President, Harry Truman, gradually came to the realization that the U.S., not the UN, would have to take the lead role in organizing post-war security.

Even before the war had ended, there were some U.S. observers who understood that this time the United States could not again withdraw across the oceans to its insular position and let events in Europe and Asia take their course without U.S. involvement. William Bullitt, who had been the U.S. Ambassador to the Soviet Union and France during the 1930s, presciently warned President Roosevelt in *1943* that our Soviet ally would likely become a threatening adversary after the war.[8] In 1944, James Burnham, then working for the Office of Strategic Services (OSS), wrote a prophetic analysis of Soviet post-war intentions.[9] In 1942, and again in 1944, Yale political scientist Nicholas Spykman wrote brilliant book-length treatises on the need for the United States to remain an active participant in the European and Asian balances of power. "It will be cheaper in the long run," Spykman wrote in 1942, "to remain a working member of the Eur[asian] power zone than to withdraw for short intermissions to our insular domain only to be forced to apply later the whole of our national strength to redress a balance that might have needed but a slight weight at the beginning." [10] The popular journalist Walter Lippmann, in his 1943 classic, *U.S. Foreign Policy: Shield of the Republic*, explained that "the strategic defenses of the United States...extend across both oceans and to all transoceanic lands from which an attack by sea or by air can be launched." America's security, argued Lippmann, "has always...extended to the coastline of Europe, Africa and Asia."[11]

It was not until after the war, however, that the Truman administration, reacting to Soviet threats to Iran, Greece, Turkey, West Berlin and elsewhere, adopted the policy of Containment, which remained the principal U.S. national security doctrine until the 1980s. Containment's leading theorist at the time was the head of the State Department's Policy Planning Staff, George F. Kennan, whose article in *Foreign Affairs*, "The Sources of Soviet Conduct" (written anonymously as "X" in 1947), had a dramatic and lasting impact on official Washington.

If Kennan was the intellectual "father" of Containment, the doctrine's intellectual "grandfather" was the British geographer, Sir Halford Mackinder. Beginning in 1904, and continuing until 1943, Mackinder developed and refined a geopolitical theory that identified the northern-central core area of Eurasia as the potential seat of a world empire. In 1943, in an article in *Foreign Affairs* entitled "The Round World and the Winning of the Peace," Mackinder envisioned a North Atlantic security alliance (he called it the Midland Ocean) that would balance Soviet power in Eurasia. Mackinder's ideas and concepts were extensively discussed on both sides of the Atlantic in the immediate post-war period.[12]

Containment manifested itself in resistance to Soviet probes in northern Iran and the Straits, the Marshall Plan, the Truman Doctrine, the Berlin Airlift, and the formation of the North Atlantic Treaty Organization (NATO). NATO committed the United States to the military defense of Western Europe. United States military forces would be stationed in Europe to bolster European defenses against possible Soviet attack, and to symbolically and practically link the security destinies of Western Europe and America. Later, the United States signed a treaty committing it to the defense of Japan, and organized security alliances, such as SEATO and CENTO to contain Soviet expansion in other areas of Eurasia.

The Containment doctrine, however, did not go unchallenged in the United States. Walter Lippmann argued that the doctrine was too broad, committing the United States to spread its resources too thinly around the periphery of Eurasia. Not every region along the periphery of the Soviet Union, Lippmann contended, was equally worthy of U.S. protection. Lippmann urged a more selective version of Containment, resisting Soviet encroachments only in those areas vital to U.S. security interests. Kennan soon made it clear that he had not argued for containment's worldwide application. He sought only to deny the Soviet Union's domination of any other of the centers of military and industrial power, variously defined as Western Europe, Britain, Japan, and the Middle East.

James Burnham, on the other hand, argued that Containment did not go far enough. In three books written between 1947 and 1951, Burnham urged U.S. policymakers to adopt a more offensive-oriented strategy that he labeled "Liberation." The goal of U.S. foreign policy, Burnham argued, should be to undermine Soviet rule in Eastern and Central Europe, and ultimately within Russia itself. This theme was picked-up by the Eisenhower administration which in its early years paid lip service to a policy of "rolling-back" communism as an alternative to Containment. When it came to reacting to actual events, however, such as the Korean War stalemate of the early 1950s and the Hungarian uprising in 1956, Eisenhower settled for Containment.

The Korean War was the first and most important test of whether Containment would give way to Liberation or "rollback." General Douglas MacArthur's brilliantly conceived and executed amphibious landing at Inchon in September 1950, provided the United States with its first real opportunity to liberate a territory (North Korea) from communist rule. At first, the liberation of North Korea was the official policy of the Truman administration, and U.S. and allied forces crossed the 38th Parallel in a drive to the Yalu River. When Chinese communist forces massively intervened in the war in October 1950, however, Truman effectively reinstated the doctrine of Containment, and both he and Eisenhower sought a return to the *status quo ante*.

Although Kennan's "X" article provided the public rationale for Containment, the classified intellectual rationale for the doctrine was contained in NSC-68, perhaps the most important national security document in the early Cold War years. NSC-68 was drafted by a committee of State Department and Pentagon staffers headed by Paul Nitze, who succeeded Kennan as State's Director of Policy and Planning. The document defined the policy of Containment as, "one which seeks by all means short of war to (1) block further expansion of Soviet Power, (2) expose the falsities of Soviet pretensions, (3) induce a retraction of the Kremlin's control and influence and (4) in general, so foster the seeds of destruction within the Soviet system that the Kremlin is brought to the point of modifying its behavior to conform to generally accepted international standards."[13] The Soviet Union, according to the report, sought world domination, and its immediate efforts were "directed toward the domination of the Eurasian land mass."[14]

NSC-68 repeatedly stressed the central importance of preventing the Soviet Union from gaining effective political control of Eurasia. This emphasis on the importance of Eurasia to U.S. security was directly traceable to Mackinder's geopolitical theories. Thus, Containment's immediate focus were the geographical regions of Eurasia that were not subject to Moscow's political control, but that could fall to Soviet or Soviet allies without U.S. support. Indeed, throughout the Cold War, the regions of Western Europe, the Middle East, and East Asia were the crucial battlegrounds.

To effectively contain Soviet Russia, NSC-68 recommended a build-up of conventional and atomic forces, as well as political, economic and psychological warfare against the Soviet Empire. It was not NSC-68, however, that produced the massive military build-up of the United States during the early 1950s; the war in Korea did that. The Korean War was the first of two "limited wars" in Asia (Vietnam was the other) that severely tested the staying power of the Containment doctrine. The Korean War also established a precedent in favor of a more passive approach to Containment than was discussed in NSC-68.

During the next thirty years, the United States for the most part hewed to an approach to Containment that attempted to counter Soviet or Soviet-directed thrusts around the world, but did not attempt aggressively to weaken or undermine the Soviet Empire. One main reason for the United States' passive approach to Containment was the nuclear stalemate. The fact that each superpower possessed increasingly destructive arsenals of nuclear weapons acted to limit the risks that both superpowers were willing to run to achieve their geopolitical aims. Cold War crises that might otherwise have led to a global hot war, such as the Hungarian uprising and Suez crisis of 1956, the Berlin crises of the late 1950s and early 1960s, the Cuban missile crisis of 1962, the war in Southeast Asia, the Czech uprising of 1968, the Arab-Israeli War of 1973, and the Soviet-Afghan War of the 1980s, were resolved, settled or ended without a direct U.S.-Soviet clash.

Another reason for America's passive approach to Containment was the hope, first expressed by Kennan in the "X" article, and repeated in NSC-68, that successful resistance to aggressive Soviet moves would cause, in Kennan's words, a "gradual mellowing" of the Soviet system. Indeed, to some, the events of the 1980s that led to the collapse of the Soviet Empire confirmed Kennan's prescience. In this interpretation, more than forty years of "firm and vigilant" Containment produced the dramatic events of 1989-1991 that ended Soviet rule in Eastern and Central Europe, and within Russia itself.

It has become increasingly evident, however, that the U.S. national security doctrine changed in the 1980s from passive Containment to a more aggressive policy of Liberation. A close scrutiny of President Reagan's speeches, interviews with national security officials, and, most important, declassified national security memoranda demonstrate that the Reagan administration pursued policies designed to bring down the Soviet Empire. For example, in January 1983, President Reagan signed National Security Decision Directive 75 (NSDD-75) which stated that U.S. policy toward the Soviet Union was "[t]o contain and over time reverse Soviet expansionism...,[t]o promote...the process of change in the Soviet Union toward a more pluralistic political and economic system in which the power of the privileged ruling elite is gradually reduced." NSDD-75 further stated that the U.S. "should exploit" a number of "vulnerabilities within the Soviet empire...," and attempt to "loosen Moscow's hold" on Eastern Europe.[15]

As Peter Schweizer, among others, has persuasively argued, Reagan's policies, including aid to anti-communist rebels in Afghanistan, Nicaragua and elsewhere, support for dissident groups and movements in Eastern Europe, the toppling of a communist government in Grenada, the denial to the Soviets of militarily useful technology, SDI, the military build-up, and efforts to exploit Soviet economic vulnerabilities, should be viewed in the context of this overall strategy.[16] As I have argued elsewhere, Reagan's approach to national security bore a remarkable resemblance to the approach recommended by James Burnham in the late 1940s-early 1950s.[17]

The end of the Cold War produced a search for a new doctrine to meet the changed national security needs of the United States. With no peer competitor to counter, the Clinton administration promoted trade, expanding economic relations with other countries, counter-proliferation efforts, nation-building, humanitarian intervention, and assertive multilateralism. This decade of relative peace and prosperity for the United States produced no overall national security doctrine that dominated policymaking.

The terrorist attacks of September 11, 2001 changed all that. In response to those attacks and to intelligence information concerning North Korean, Iraqi and Iranian efforts to obtain weapons of mass destruction, the George W. Bush administration adopted a new national security doctrine, popularly called "Preemption." Bush set forth the new doctrine one year after the September 11 attacks in a document entitled "The National Security Strategy of the United States."

The new strategy envisions a long, complex struggle against global terrorists and the states that support or harbor them. Of special concern are those "rogue" states that have or are attempting to acquire weapons of mass destruction. As Bush explained, "We are menaced less by fleets and armies than by catastrophic technologies in the hands of the embittered few." The United States, according to the new doctrine, will "prevent our enemies from threatening us, our allies, and our friends, with weapons of mass destruction."

In the past, the United States could rely on its insular location and industrial capacity to marshal its resources to respond to attacks by its enemies. But in the wake of the September 11 attacks and the ability of rogue states to acquire weapons of mass destruction, "the United States can no longer solely rely on a reactive posture as we have in the past....We cannot let our enemies strike first." To prevent or forestall nuclear, chemical or biological weapons attacks by terrorists "of global reach" and/or rogue states, "the United States will, if necessary, act preemptively."

The U.S. war against Islamic terrorists and the Taliban regime in Afghanistan was not waged as part of the new strategy. That war was undertaken in reaction to the September 11 attacks. The U.S. and coalition attack on, and invasion of, Iraq in 2003 was the first manifestation of the Preemption doctrine. The Bush administration, in justifying its attack on Iraq, pointed to Saddam Hussein's connection to and support of terrorism, and his nuclear, chemical and biological weapons programs. Contrary to the assertions of many of his critics, Bush did not claim that Iraq's threat to use or transfer such weapons to terrorists was "imminent." In fact, the rationale behind the Preemption doctrine is that the United States can no longer afford to wait until such threats are imminent. The U.S., the new doctrine states, will defend its "interests at home and abroad by identifying and destroying the threat before it reaches our borders." And again, "We must be prepared to stop rogue states and their terrorist clients before they are able to threaten or use weapons of mass destruction against the United States and our allies and friends."

The new doctrine of Preemption also makes clear that, though the United States prefers to act with its allies, it will act alone, if necessary, to prevent more September 11th type attacks. "[W]e will not hesitate to act alone...," states the new document, "to exercise our right of self-defense by acting preemptively against such terrorists, to prevent them from doing harm against our people and our country."

Thus, in the span of 227 years, United States national security doctrine has evolved from a policy of distant, and detached, and a sometimes not so well armed neutrality to unilaterally taking preemptive military action anywhere in the world. This evolution in policy is a reflection of both the growth, in size and power, of the United States (in absolute and relative terms), the gradual geopolitical shrinking of the globe, and the nature of the threats the U.S. now faces.

Only time will tell whether the new doctrine of Preemption will survive the increasingly controversial war against Iraq. The Bush administration is under fire for allegedly exaggerating the threat that Iraq posed to U.S. national security before the war, and for failing to anticipate and plan for the difficulties of post-war occupation and administration of Iraq. Moreover, the specter of applying Preemption to North Korea and Iran, countries that have acquired or are attempting to acquire weapons of mass destruction and that provide support for terrorist groups, is especially worrisome to some observers. Preemption, it is argued, clashes with the prudent counsel of Secretary of State John Quincy Adams that America should not go abroad in search of monsters to destroy.

Those who support Preemption contend, however, that the monsters abroad have demonstrated the ability to inflict great harm on the United States, and could do even greater harm if armed with weapons of mass destruction. Preemption's supporters admit that the new doctrine is a significant departure from previous national security policies, but they argue that such a departure is justified by the nature and magnitude of the threat.

Stationing large numbers of American troops in Europe and Asia during peacetime during the Cold War to effectuate Containment, the supporters of Preemption point out, also was a radical departure from previous national security policies, but that departure, too, was justified by the nature and magnitude of the (Soviet) threat.

The evolution of American national security doctrines demonstrates that U.S. policymakers repeatedly have reacted to immediate national security threats or challenges with far-sighted, long-term but pragmatic doctrines that have helped them steer the ship-of-state through the troubled and uncertain waters of international politics. We can only hope that in fashioning the new national security doctrine, the Bush administration proves to be as pragmatic, prudent and far-sighted as its predecessors.

ENDNOTES

1. For example, the Truman Doctrine (aid to Greece and Turkey under assault by communist forces after world War II), the Nixon Doctrine (military aid to key countries in strategic areas of the world as a substitute for direct U.S. military intervention), the Carter Doctrine (announcing that the U.S. will defend its interests in the Persian Gulf region), and the Reagan Doctrine (aid to anti-communist forces throughout the world in communist controlled countries).

2. Mahan expressed these sentiments in books, articles and letters during 1890-1914. His views on the impact of Washington's Farewell Address and other aspects of American foreign policy are described in my introductions to Mahan's *The Problem of Asia: Its Effect upon International Politics* and *The Interest of America in International Conditions*, which were recently reprinted by Transaction Publishers.

3. Felix Gilbert, *The Beginnings of American Foreign Policy: To the Farewell Address* (New York: Harper Torchbooks, 1961), p. 135.

4. Eugene V. Rostow, *A Breakfast for Bonaparte: U.S. National Security Interests from the Heights of Abraham to the Nuclear Age* (Washington, D.C.: National Defense University Press, 1993), p. 112.

5. Thomas A. Bailey, *A Diplomatic History of the American People* (New York: Meredith Corporation, 1969), pp. 526-527.

6. Alfred Thayer Mahan, *The Interest of America in International Conditions* (New Brunswick, N.J.: Transaction Publishers, 2003) with a new introduction by Francis P. Sempa. This is a recently released reprint of the original work.

7. Winston S. Churchill, *The Gathering Storm* (Boston: Houghton Mifflin Company, 1948), p. 17.

8. Bullitt's life and diplomatic career are examined in Francis P. Sempa, "William C. Bullitt: Diplomat and Prophet," *American Diplomacy* (January 2003), www.americandiplomacy.org.

9. Burnham's writings on the Cold War are examined in chapter 4 of Francis P. Sempa, *Geopolitics: From the Cold War to the 21st Century* (New Brunswick, N.J.: Transaction Publishers, 2002), pp. 39-63.

10. Nicholas Spykman, *America's Strategy in World Politics* (New York: Harcourt, Brace & Co., 1942), pp. 467-468. Spykman's other book on this topic was *The Geography of the Peace* (New York: Harcourt, Brace &Co., 1944).

11. Boston: Little Brown and Co., 1943, pp. 94-95.

12. Mackinder's geopolitical writings are examined in Francis P. Sempa, *Geopolitics: From the Cold War to the 21st Century* (New Brunswick, N.J.: Transaction Publishers, 2002), pp. 9-37, 67-72, 91-92.

13. *NSC-68: A Report to the National Security Council on United States Objectives and Programs for National Security*, reprinted from the May-June 1975 issue of the *Naval War College Review*, p. 68.

14. *Ibid.*, p. 54. John Lewis Gaddis' *Strategies of Containment* is a useful discussion of containment's varied applications.

15. Christopher Simpson, *National Security Directives of the Reagan and Bush Administrations* (Boulder, Colo.: Westview Press, 1995), pp. 255-263.

16. Peter Schweizer, *Victory: The Reagan Administration's Secret Strategy That Hastened the Collapse of the Soviet Union* (New York: Atlantic Monthly Press, 1994).

17. Francis P. Sempa, *Geopolitics: From the Cold War to the 21st Century* (New Brunswick, N.J.: Transaction Publishers, 2002), pp. 58-59.

Trafalgar and the Balance of Power

Nearly two hundred years ago, October 21, 1805, one of the most important naval battles in world history was fought in waters off the coast of Cadiz, Spain near Cape Trafalgar. The British fleet, commanded by Admiral Horatio Nelson, defeated a combined French-Spanish fleet in a ferocious six-hour battle that ended Napoleon Bonaparte's chances of successfully invading England.

Trafalgar was one of those rare battles that truly affected significantly the course of world history. Bonaparte, though he won victory after victory on the continent of Europe in the early 1800s, knew that his goal of an ever-expanding French Empire would be frustrated unless he could defeat or neutralize the opposition of Great Britain. "Make us masters of the [English] channel," he told his admirals, "and we are masters of the world."

Indeed, it is arguable that French world rule hinged upon the outcome of the Battle of Trafalgar. Shortly before Trafalgar, Napoleon's army defeated the Austrians at Ulm. Less than two months after Trafalgar, the French defeated the Russian Army at Austerlitz. Upon hearing of the Russian loss at Austerlitz, British Prime Minister William Pitt commented, "Roll up the map of Europe; it will not be needed for the next ten years." The next year, Napoleon beat the Prussians at Jena and Auerstadt. In June 1807, the French Army again defeated the Russians at Friedland, forcing the Tsar into an alliance with Napoleon formalized in the Treaty of Tilsit on July 7, 1807.

The Treaty of Tilsit, wrote Winston Churchill in his *History of the English Speaking Peoples*, "was the culmination of Napoleon's power." The French Emperor dominated virtually all of Europe. "Only Britannia remained," wrote Churchill, "unreconciled, unconquered, implacable. There she lay in her Island, mistress of the seas and oceans...facing this immense combination alone, sullen, fierce, and almost unperturbed."

Had the combined French-Spanish fleet on that October day in 1805 destroyed or captured the British fleet, leading to the conquest or neutralization of England, by 1807 France would have eliminated all effective opposition to its power on the Eurasian land mass, and would have been free to turn her whole strength toward the Western Hemisphere, including the United States. The United States would have been unable to resist a French Empire that was uncontested in Europe and that was supreme both on land and at sea.

Some American statesmen of the time recognized the potential danger to U.S. security. Alexander Hamilton in 1798 warned in a series of newspaper articles that the French Empire had "swelled to a gigantic size," aimed at "the control of mankind," and endeavored "to become the Tyrant both of Sea and Land." The British Navy, argued Hamilton, "has repeatedly upheld the balance of power, in opposition to the grasping ambition of France,...[and] has been more than once an effectual shield against real danger." One year after Trafalgar, Fisher Ames wrote that "a peace...that should humble England, and withdraw her navy from any further opposition to [Napoleon's] arms, would give the civilized world a master" with "the weight and ignominy of a new Roman dominion." Congressman John Randolph, in an effort to dissuade his colleagues from voting for war with Britain in 1812, asked rhetorically, "Suppose France in possession of British naval power; what would be your condition? What could you expect if [the French] were the uncontrolled lords of the ocean?" President Thomas Jefferson, referring to Napoleon after Trafalgar and Austerlitz, expressed the wish that "he who has armies may not have the Dominion of the sea," and later warned that it was not in the United States' interest "that all of Europe should be reduced to a single monarchy....Surely none of us wish to see Bonaparte conquer Russia and lay thus at his feet the whole continent of Europe. This done, England would be but a breakfast....Put all Europe into [Napoleon's] hands, and he might spare such a force to be sent in British ships as I would as leave not have to encounter."

Such sound geopolitical reasoning, however, was overtaken by the fear and anger of Americans produced by harsh British commercial and trade restrictions, seizures of U.S. ships, and impressments of U.S. seamen to serve on British warships. Even with the rising anti-British sentiment, however, the vote for war against Britain in 1812 passed by only thirty votes in the House of Representatives and only six votes in the Senate. Remarkably, a proposal simultaneously to declare war on France was defeated in the Senate by just four votes!

Perhaps fortunately for the United States and the world, the British victory at Trafalgar denied to Napoleon the one missing element of his plan for world hegemony — supremacy at sea. Unable to directly defeat Britain militarily, Napoleon attempted to starve her into submission by instituting the "Continental System," a policy designed to close off the European continent to British trade. But Britain used her sea power to circumvent the Continental System, insert an army on the Iberian Peninsula (partly under the command of Arthur Wellesley, the future Duke of Wellington), and to encourage and support the formation of yet another coalition to fight Napoleon.

That coalition proved to be the instrument of Napoleon's downfall. French losses on the Iberian Peninsula during 1808-1814 (a theater of war that Napoleon called the "Spanish ulcer") coupled with Napoleon's disastrous invasion of Russia in 1812 led to the French Emperor's defeat and exile to Elba. His subsequent escape from Elba and attempt to restore his empire in Europe came to an end in a bloody battle near a Belgian village called Waterloo.

Napoleon was again exiled, this time to the more isolated island of St. Helena. The peacemakers at Vienna constructed the "Concert of Europe" which worked to avoid another general European war and to uphold the European balance of power.

The British victory at Trafalgar contained Napoleon's conquests to Europe, and made possible his ultimate defeat. In effect, the British navy protected the United States from Napoleon's dreams of world hegemony. The great American naval historian Alfred Thayer Mahan was surely correct when he wrote about Trafalgar that it was "those far distant, storm-beaten ships...[that] stood between [France] and the dominion of the world."

Visionaries of the American Empire: Hamilton and Mahan

The idea of an American "empire" is not new to the twenty-first century. In fact, it is as old as the Republic itself. What some today call the "American Empire" emerged gradually and in two separate phases. The first phase began immediately after the War of Independence and lasted until the late nineteenth century. The second phase began around the time of the Spanish-American War in 1898 and continues to this day. Each phase of empire began with an idea championed by brilliant, articulate, and persuasive proponents.

One proponent was an illegitimate child born on an island in the Caribbean Sea who came to the American colonies, fought in the War of Independence, wrote insightful and influential articles about the structure of the new United States' government, financial institutions, and commercial industries, advised the President of the United States, and rose to the high office of Treasury Secretary. The other was born on the grounds of the U.S. Military Academy at West Point, fought in the American Civil War, wrote brilliant articles and books about naval history and strategy, advised the President of the United States, and rose to the rank of Rear Admiral in the U.S. Navy. Respectively, their visions and ideas provided the intellectual foundations for the 13 original American states to expand into a continental empire in the nineteenth century, and for that continental empire to emerge as a global superpower in the twentieth century.

Alexander Hamilton rose to positions of prominence and influence by sheer force of intellect and remarkable administrative skills. Theodore Roosevelt called him "the most brilliant American statesman who ever lived, possessing the loftiest and keenest intellect of his time."[1] He was, wrote biographer Ron Chernow, "at once a thinker and doer, sparkling theoretician and masterful executive."[2] George Washington found him indispensable as a military aid during the War of Independence and as an advisor during his two terms as President. As author of most of the *Federalist Papers*, he persuaded his countrymen of the need for a strong central government and a powerful chief executive. As Washington's Treasury Secretary he launched the new nation on the road to financial and commercial growth and expansion. As the President's chief foreign policy advisor, he helped Washington steer a careful course of neutrality between our old adversary Great Britain and our old ally France, so that the new nation could survive, grow, and prosper instead of intervening in European conflicts.

Hamilton's approach to economic and foreign policy was based on his belief and hope that the United States could emerge as a great empire, rivaling, and someday surpassing, the empire of Great Britain. Indeed, Great Britain was his model for shaping U.S. economic policies and institutions. Hamilton greatly admired the British Empire for its unparalleled financial and commercial power and its preeminent global position. As Treasury Secretary he generously borrowed British financial practices and encouraged trade with our former colonial masters and wartime antagonist. As chief foreign policy advisor to

President Washington, he counseled cooperation with Britain, focused on the common security interests of Britain and the U.S., and advocated the development of strong U.S. naval power.

In 1795, Hamilton described his country as the "embryo of a great empire."[3] Even before the American Revolution, Hamilton predicted that "in fifty or sixty years, America will be in no need of protection from Great Britain. She will then be able to protect herself, both at home and abroad. She will have plenty of men and a plenty of materials to provide and equip a formidable navy."[4]

Hamilton's vision of empire extended to the entire Western Hemisphere. In *Federalist 11*, he wrote that the nation's "situation" and "interests" prompt it to "aim at an ascendant in the system of American affairs," and he advocated "erecting one great American system, superior to the control of all transatlantic force or influence, and able to dictate the terms of the connection between the old and the new world."

Hamilton was an early proponent of what was later called America's "Manifest Destiny;" the idea that the United States would expand from the Atlantic coast to the Pacific Ocean. As early as 1798, Hamilton called for the annexation of all the territories east of the Mississippi, including Florida.[5] Later, when President Jefferson was negotiating for the Louisiana territory, Hamilton urged him to be more aggressive and "energetic" in preventing French control of the Mississippi.[6]

The United States during most of the nineteenth century pursued and achieved Hamilton's vision of a continental empire and a dominant position in the Western Hemisphere. That remarkable achievement resulted not just from Hamilton's idea of an American Empire, but also from the financial and commercial dynamism and energy he set in motion as our nation's first Treasury Secretary. As Ron Chernow concluded, "No other founder articulated such a clear and prescient vision of America's future political, military, and economic strength or crafted such ingenious mechanisms to bind the nation together."[7] "Today," wrote Chernow, "we are indisputably the heirs to Hamilton's America..."[8]

By the late nineteenth century, the United States had achieved hegemony over the center of North America from the Atlantic Ocean to the Pacific Ocean and from Canada to the Gulf of Mexico. The American Empire stretched from "sea to shining sea." This was the same time period when the great powers of Europe were busy conquering and governing colonial empires in Africa, Asia, and elsewhere. Would the United States join in the struggle for empire? Should the United States join in the struggle for empire?

In 1890, eight years before the Spanish-American War propelled the U.S. to construct an overseas empire, a little-known navy captain named Alfred Thayer Mahan wrote a book entitled *The Influence of Sea Power upon History 1660-1783*.[9] The book was an international sensation and gained for Mahan national and international fame and recognition. It was translated into several foreign languages and was avidly studied by the navies of all the major powers. It was Mahan's second book[10] and launched him on a prolific writing career as the author of books and articles on naval history and strategy, and international relations.

Mahan had served on naval vessels during the Civil War and later taught at the Naval War College in Newport, Rhode Island. Mahan's study of history, especially the history of the British navy and empire, convinced him that sea power was the key to national greatness and prosperity.

Like Hamilton, he admired the British Empire and believed that the United States and Great Britain had common security interests. As early as 1890, in an article in the *Atlantic Monthly*, Mahan urged U.S. policymakers to come to a "cordial understanding" with Great Britain because both nations had "a similarity of character and ideas" that would eventually result in "co-operation beneficial to both."[11] Four years later, Mahan wrote an article for the *North American Review* entitled, "The Possibilities of an Anglo-American Reunion." In that article, he wrote, "'To Great Britain and the United States…is intrusted (sic) a maritime interest in the broadest sense of the word, which demands, as one of the conditions of its exercise and its safety, the organized force adequate to control the general course of events at sea…'"[12]

Though initially an isolationist, Mahan, after reading Theodore Mommsen's multi-volume *The History of Rome* and researching Great Britain's use of sea power to construct and expand its empire, converted to a strong proponent of imperialism.[13] In a letter written in 1896, Mahan opined that "the time has come…when [the U.S.] should and must count for something in the affairs of the world at large." A hundred years ago, he continued, the U.S. policy of isolation was "wise and imperative," but now it was time to "take our share in the turmoil of the world…."[14]

Mahan, like Hamilton, called for a strong navy. He advocated the annexation of Hawaii, and later the Philippine Islands. The United States had to play a greater role in the world because the world was getting "smaller." "Though distant," Mahan explained, "our shores can be reached."[15]

Mahan also advocated the construction of an inter-oceanic canal across the Central American isthmus which would foster U.S. control of the Caribbean Sea maritime region and enable our navy to more readily transit between the Atlantic and Pacific Oceans.

Mahan's writings eventually brought him to the attention of Assistant Secretary of the Navy and future President Theodore Roosevelt. Roosevelt shared Mahan's views that the United States needed to play a larger role in the world and consequently required a stronger navy. Mahan and Roosevelt began a correspondence in 1888 that continued until Mahan's death in 1914. In these remarkable letters, the two men discussed naval strategy, history, and international relations. In one letter, Roosevelt told Mahan that he had studied his books "to pretty good purpose."[16] Mahan did not have a permanent official position in Roosevelt's administration, and he did not influence Roosevelt to the extent that Hamilton influenced Washington. But Mahan did exert a significant influence on Roosevelt's thinking concerning naval strategy and America's position in the world.

Mahan's influence, however, like Hamilton's, extended beyond the President he advised to the entire nation and to future American statesmen. Mahan envisioned the United States as the geopolitical successor to the British Empire, exerting its financial, military, and political influence to advance its interests and maintain the global balance of power. In *The Interest of America in International Conditions* (1910), Mahan warned of the growing menace to the balance of power posed by Wilhelmine Germany and advocated a U.S. alliance with Britain, France, and Russia to offset German power. In *The Problem of Asia* (1905), Mahan envisioned a maritime alliance between the U.S., Britain, France, Germany, and Japan to counter Russian land power in the heart of Asia (a remarkable prediction of the post-World War II U.S. policy of containment).

Fareed Zakaria called Mahan "the most prominent intellectual figure to advocate expansion" in nineteenth century America.[17] Walter LaFeber placed Mahan among the strategists who "led the United States into the international power politics of the early twentieth century."[18] Margaret Sprout wrote that Mahan "played a leading role in persuading the United States to pursue a larger destiny overseas during the opening years of the twentieth century."[19] Charles Hubbard called Mahan "an influential promoter of United States naval and commercial expansion during America's rise to world power in the late nineteenth century."[20] Hans Weigert claimed that Mahan "preached the gospel of the new American Imperialism drawing its strength from sea power, and a new Manifest Destiny based on America's future role as the leading maritime nation in the world."[21]

America's place in the world today is much as it was envisioned by Hamilton and Mahan. Both believed that it was the destiny of the United States to expand, prosper, and play a leading role in world affairs. By a remarkable historical coincidence, these brilliant and prolific men attained the height of their influence at important turning points in American history. Hamilton's ideas profoundly influenced the nation as it emerged from its War of Independence, formed governing institutions, and began to move forward as an independent and growing country. Mahan's ideas profoundly influenced the nation as it moved from consolidating its control of the continent to find its role in the larger world.

ENDNOTES

1. Quoted in Ron Chernow, *Alexander Hamilton* (New York: The Penguin Press 2004), p. 4.

2. Chernow, *Alexander Hamilton*, p. 4.

3. Robert Kagan, "Our Messianic Impulse," *Washington Post*, December 10, 2006 http://www.carnegieendowment.org/publications/index.cfm?fa=view&id=18908&prog=zg p&proj=zusr

4. Robert Kagan, *Dangerous Nation: America's Place in the World from Its Earliest Days to the Dawn of the Twentieth Century* (New York: Alfred A. Knopf, 2006), p. 37.

5. Chernow, *Alexander Hamilton*, p. 566.

6. Robert W. Tucker and David C. Hendrickson, *Empire of Liberty: The Statecraft of Thomas Jefferson* (New York: Oxford University Press, 1990), p. 91.

7. Chernow, *Alexander Hamilton*, p. 4.

8. Chernow, *Alexander Hamilton*, p. 6.

9. First published in the U.S. by Little Brown & Co., Boston, Mass.

10. His first book was a study of naval action during the Civil War, *The Gulf and Inland Waters*.

11. A.T. Mahan, "The United States Looking Outward," in *The Interest of America in Sea Power Present and Future* (London: Sampson Low, Marston & Co., 1898). First published in the *Atlantic Monthly* in 1890.

12. The article was reprinted in Mahan's book, *The Interest of America in Sea Power Present and Future*, p. 111.

13. For an exhaustive analysis of Mahan's writings on international relations and geopolitics, see my lengthy introductions to Mahan's *The Problem of Asia: Its Effect upon International Politics* (New Brunswick, NJ: Transaction Publishers, 2003), Introduction by Francis P. Sempa, pp. 1-49 and Mahan's *The Interest of America in International Conditions* (New Brunswick, NJ: Transaction Publishers, 2003), Introduction by Francis P. Sempa, pp. 1-37.

14. Mahan to James R. Thursfield, January 10, 1896, in Robert Seager II and Dorothy Maguire, eds., *The Letters and Papers of Alfred Thayer Mahan*, vol. II (Annapolis, MD: Naval Institute Press, 1975), p. 442.

15. Mahan, "The United States Looking Outward," in *The Interest of America in Sea Power*, p. 18.

16. The Mahan-Roosevelt correspondence is studied and collected in Richard W. Turk's, *The Ambiguous Relationship: Theodore Roosevelt and Alfred Thayer Mahan* (New York: Greenwood Press, 1987).

17. Fareed Zakaria, *From Wealth to Power: The Unusual Origins of America's World Role* (Princeton, NJ: Princeton University Press, 1998), p. 134.

18. Walter LaFeber, *The New Empire: An Interpretation of American Expansion 1860-1898* (Ithaca, NY: Cornell University Press, 1963), p. 101.

19. "Mahan: Evangelist of Sea Power," in Anthony W. Gray and Elston T. White, eds., *Military Strategy* (Washington, DC: National Defense University Press, 1983), pp. 39-40.

20. Charles M. Hubbard, "Alfred Thayer Mahan: The Reluctant Seaman," *American History* (August 1998).

21. Hans Weigert, et al., *Principles of Political Geography* (New York: Appleton-Century-Crofts, Inc., 1957), p. 212.

Sea Power and Capitalism

Although you would not guess it from reading the major daily newspapers and weekly news magazines or watching television news shows and documentaries, American foreign policy has been remarkably successful during its 230-year history. Most of what passes for "journalism" today, unfortunately, has a very narrow and unhistorical focus which tends to distort reality. America's success in the "big picture" of history is often obscured by reporting and analysis of the minutia of individual foreign policy problems and failures. Popular journalism shows us some of the trees, but not the forest.

To be sure, the United States throughout its history has suffered its share of costly setbacks and failures—the pillaging of U.S. ships by the Barbary pirates; the burning of its capital during the War of 1812; a string of early military defeats in the Civil War; the Philippine insurrection after the Spanish-American War; the attempts at arms limitation, utopian peace agreements, and appeasement of dictators between World Wars I and II; the intelligence and diplomatic debacle that resulted in the successful Japanese attack on Pearl Harbor; the early military fiascos in North Africa in the Second World War; the failure to prevent Soviet domination of Eastern and Central Europe following World War II; the loss of China to the communists; the Korean stalemate; the damage to NATO resulting from the Suez crisis of 1956; the U-2 incident; the fall of Cuba to communism; the Bay of Pigs fiasco; defeat in the Vietnam War; the loss of allies in Nicaragua and Iran in the late 1970s; the Iranian hostage crisis; the destruction of the Marine barracks in Lebanon in the early 1980s; the Iran-Contra scandal; the 9/11 attacks on New York and the Pentagon; and the difficulties posed by the current Iraqi insurgency—but, in the long run, the United States has emerged victorious and stronger after every great global challenge.

Walter Russell Mead, the Henry A. Kissinger Senior Fellow in U.S. Foreign Policy at the Council on Foreign Relations, in his new book *God and Gold: Britain, America and the Making of the Modern World*, takes a "big picture" view of U.S. foreign policy, and finds the roots and success of that policy in British history and a unique Anglo-American geopolitical approach to the world. Mead's book is in many respects a throwback to the broad, general geopolitical works of writers such as Halford Mackinder, Nicholas Spykman, and Alfred Thayer Mahan. Like those intellectual forbearers, Mead presents a sweeping overview of Anglo-American foreign policy within the broad context of four centuries of global history.

For Mead, the inescapable historical geopolitical truth is that, "in three hundred years of warfare, the English-speaking powers keep winning....[E]ither the British or the Americans or both have been on the winning side of every major war in which they have participated since the late seventeenth century." Beginning with the Hapsburg Empire of Charles V and Phillip II, a series of would-be European or Eurasian hegemons threatened to upset the global balance of power, but were ultimately frustrated and defeated by British-led coalitions, and later American-led coalitions. Louis XIV, Revolutionary and Napoleonic France, Wilhelmine Germany and Nazi Germany, and, most recently, the Soviet Union, all met the same dismal fate at the hands of Anglo-American power. The bulk of Mead's book is an effort to explain the remarkable success story of Anglo-American foreign policy.

That Anglo-American global success, according to Mead, is, fundamentally, the result of two factors: capitalism and sea power. Over three centuries, the English-speaking powers constructed, exploited, and dominated a global financial system that made them generally more prosperous and more technologically advanced than other societies. They developed and sustained sophisticated methods of banking, transportation, trade, marketing, investment, public and private credit, and debt financing, operating within a complex financial infrastructure and legal system, that produced remarkable commercial expansion, wealth, and technological and scientific innovation, all of which enabled the Anglo-American powers repeatedly to build and sustain powerful military forces and to extend financial support to crucial allies in global conflicts.

Mead is not the first observer to identify this important ingredient of Anglo-American global success. In his masterful book *Democratic Ideals and Reality* (1919), Mackinder examined it at length in discussing the importance to successful great powers of what he called "social momentum." Productive, innovative, wealth-producing societies, Mackinder wrote, are "Going Concerns," whose organizers and administrators help maintain and channel the resources--human and material--of society to sustain and increase the relative power position of that society in the world at large. Mackinder believed that the steady, relentless advance of the "social organism" was essential to the geopolitical success of nations.

The roots of British and American capitalist-driven global success, Mead contends, can be found in the unique Anglo-American culture, including its religious dimension. "The decisive factor in the success of the English-speaking world," Mead writes, "is that both the British and the Americans came from a culture that was uniquely well positioned to develop and harness the titanic forces of capitalism as they emerged on the world scene." The Anglo-American culture rewarded individual initiative and risk-taking, and more readily adapted to economic and social change than competing cultures. Adam Smith's "invisible hand" converted the self-interest of millions of individuals into growing, prosperous national economies. Meanwhile, the religious pluralism of the English-speaking peoples accommodated the dynamic aspects of capitalism, while religious devotion constrained individual appetites to help preserve social order. Mead accurately describes the Anglo-American social momentum as a "Promethean drive to acquire all the power that can be acquired, to do everything it is possible for humanity to do, to learn what can be learned, to build what can be built, and to change what can be changed..." It is this phenomenon, writes Mead, "that impelled the...maritime powers to their global position."

The second fundamental factor underlying Anglo-American geopolitical success, sea power, had its roots in the great Dutch maritime empire of the 16th and 17th centuries, which, Mead explains, relied on a navy that "dominated the oceanic trade routes of the world." Amsterdam became the financial center of the world, while "Dutch scientists and scholars astounded the world with discoveries and inventions." British sea power succeeded the Dutch, and in turn, was succeeded by the United States. The world's financial center shifted from Amsterdam to London to New York. Sea power enabled the establishment and supported the maintenance of a maritime world order.

Mead invokes Mahan to explain the broad, geopolitical meaning of sea power:

> In Mahan's sense, sea power is more than a navy. It is more than control of strategic trade routes. It means using the mobility of the seas to build a global system resting on economic links as well as on military strength. It means using the strategic flexibility of an offshore power, protected to some degree from the rivalries and hostilities of land powers surrounded by powerful neighbors, to build power strategies that other countries cannot counter. It means using command of the seas to plant colonies whose wealth and success reinforce the mother country. It involves developing a global system that is relatively easy to establish and which, once developed, proves extremely difficult to dislodge.

Here, Mead grasps the fundamental geopolitical advantage that inures to insular sea powers by virtue of their geographical position. British domination of the British Isles and U.S. domination of North America freed both powers from what Mead calls "the tyranny of neighborhood"-- challenges and distractions from land powers, and, thereby, enabled them to devote their energies outward toward the great Eurasian landmass.

Eurasia, what Mackinder in his seminal 1904 paper "The Geographical Pivot of History" called the "Great Continent," contains most of the world's people and resources. Recognizing that important geopolitical fact, British and American statesmen repeatedly sought to encourage, sustain, and reinforce a balance of power on the Eurasian landmass by, in Mead's words, "promoting the weaker states against the strongest as its allies in any geostrategic theater." In the memorable words of Sir Eyre Crowe in his famous Foreign Office Memorandum of 1907, Britain (and later, the United States) maintained its security "by throwing her weight now in this scale and now in that, but ever on the side opposed to the political dictatorship of the strongest single State or group at a given time."

The key element in the British and American promotion of the balance of power was, and is, sea power. As Mead explains, "[i]n Anglo-American strategic thought, there is one world composed of many theaters. The theaters are all linked by the sea, and whoever controls the sea can choose the architecture that shapes the world." Mahan, in his classic *The Influence of Sea Power upon History 1660-1783* (1890), compared the oceans and seas of the world to "a great highway...a wide common." Mackinder, in his book *Britain and the British Seas* (1902), reflected that "[t]he unity of the ocean is the simple physical fact underlying the dominant value of sea-power in the modern globe-wide world."

Mead's arguments for the superior value of dominant sea power throughout history are similar to those made by the strategic analyst Colin Gray in his important book, *The Leverage of Sea Power* (1992). Gray introduced that book by noting that "Great sea powers or maritime coalitions have either won or, occasionally, drawn every major war in modern history." To support his thesis about the strategic leverage of sea power, Gray used case histories from ancient times to the Cold War, and included in his analysis the same Anglo-American geopolitical struggles dating from the late 16th century that Mead discusses in *God and Gold*. Gray further expanded on this analysis two years later in *The Navy in the Post-Cold War World: The Uses and Value of Strategic Sea Power* (1994).

For Mead, capitalism plus sea power equals the "maritime order," which has been dominating the world for at least three centuries. To understand the past success and future prospects of U.S. foreign policy, Mead explains, it is necessary to view it in the context of "the long-term history of the maritime order [which] highlights the geopolitical, economic, and cultural foundations of America's global position." The broad goal of American foreign policy, therefore, should be to perpetuate that maritime order in the face of inevitable future challenges.

Mead packages his proposed grand strategy to "maintain the health and vitality of the maritime order" into five broad policies: (1) preserving our open, dynamic society at home; (2) continuing our economic, cultural, religious, and political engagement with the rest of the world; (3) preventing the emergence of another would-be hegemon in Asia by promoting a regional balance of power; (4) further integrating the American-led global economy; and (5) promoting institutions, practices, and values in strategic areas of the globe.

Despite America's current difficulties in Iraq, Mead argues that global conditions "seem broadly favorable to the continuation of a unique American global role and to the absence (or the failure) of great-power challenges to the maritime system." Europe is geopolitically quiet, while Asian geopolitics is emerging in a manner that portends a potentially stable balance of power between major powers such as China, India, Japan, and Russia, and lesser powers like Pakistan, Indonesia, and Vietnam, with the United States acting as an offshore balancer.

Mead, though highly critical of what he calls the foreign policy missteps of the George W. Bush administration in the struggle against Islamic terrorists, cautions against both apocalyptic visions of a clash of civilizations and an all-consuming despair over our current troubles in the Middle East. "[T]his is far from the greatest crisis in the long history of the maritime system," he writes. He compares the current challenge of Al-Qaeda and other Wahhabi-inspired Islamic terrorists to previous non-Islamic movements, such as the Xhosa's in southern Africa in the mid-19th century, the Shawnee followers of Tenskwatawa in early-19th century America, and the Boxers in early-20th century China, that sought to resist or challenge the maritime order. All ended up being small blips on the screen of history. Indeed, Mead, perhaps too sanguinely, envisions a growing diversity and pluralism within Islam that will enable Islamic societies to reconcile with the liberal maritime world order.

Mead concludes his profound and intellectually stimulating geopolitical analysis by urging Americans to approach the world with the wisdom and insight of the great Lutheran clergyman and intellectual, Reinhold Niebuhr. "No twentieth-century American," Mead writes about the author of *Moral Man and Immoral Society* and other great works, "so fully and completely articulated and simultaneously critiqued the core elements of the Anglo-American worldview as this intellectual Protestant clergyman." Niebuhr understood man's imperfectability, the flaws in human nature (based on the Christian doctrine of original sin) and the consequent necessity in foreign policy of frequently having to choose among evils. He was profoundly skeptical of abstract ideals and utopian schemes. He also understood that force, duplicity, and coercion were sometimes necessary elements of our nation's foreign policy. Finally, Niebuhr knew that there were no permanent, all-encompassing solutions to conflicts among peoples and nations, and, therefore, statesmen have to settle for partial victories and temporary advantages, even as they prepare to meet future challenges. "As Americans strive to understand the nature of the threat revealed by the terror attacks of 9/11 and to develop a foreign policy stance that can guide them through this latest challenge to the maritime order," Mead writes, "Niebuhr's ideas seem more compelling and vital than ever."

Since the end of the Cold War, the United States has been waiting for a new "Mr. X" to emerge from its foreign policy establishment, as George F. Kennan did in 1946-47, to set forth in vivid and persuasive prose a broad grand strategy to guide its policymakers in a dangerous and uncertain world. Walter Russell Mead, with *God and Gold*, can plausibly lay claim to Kennan's intellectual mantle. Hopefully, our nation's policymakers will react to Mead's book the way President Harry Truman and his advisors, and their successors, reacted to Kennan's "Long Telegram" and his "X" article in *Foreign Affairs* where he outlined the strategy of "containment." Our nation's future prosperity and security are at stake.

The Geopolitics of the American Civil War

It is often forgotten or overlooked that the American Civil War had important global geopolitical consequences. The war was fought during a time when the United States was aggressively pursuing its "manifest destiny" to occupy and politically control the center of North America from the Atlantic to the Pacific Ocean, from "sea to shining sea." The war's outcome would determine whether this immense territory would be home to one or two powerful countries. Looking back from the perspective of 20th century history, it is arguable that the fate of the world, not just of our own country, was at stake at Shiloh, Antietam, Vicksburg, Gettysburg, Chattanooga, Atlanta, Petersburg and Appomattox.

The three most significant geopolitical events of the 19th century were the defeat of Napoleon's French Empire, the political unification of Germany, and the rise of the United States to world power. The latter event—America's rise to great power status—depended on the outcome of the Civil War.

The United States in the first-half of the 19th century pursued three broad, complementary policies that enabled it to securely expand its territory and power. First, it followed the wise counsel of its first President, George Washington, by remaining aloof from most European conflicts. Second, it exploited Europe's rivalries in an effort to remove then exclude European powers from the Western Hemisphere (the Monroe Doctrine). Third, it opportunistically acquired territory by diplomacy (the Louisiana Purchase), war (the Mexican-American War), and the ruthless removal of native populations.

The creation of the Confederate States of America in 1861 threatened to stop "manifest destiny" dead in its tracks. An independent Confederacy that permanently split America into two strong and competing powers was an outcome of the war greatly desired by British and French statesmen of the time.

During the war, Russia's minister to England reported that, "The English Government...desires the separation of North America into two republics, which will watch each other jealously and counterbalance each other. Then England, on terms of peace and commerce with both, would have nothing to fear from either; for she would dominate them, restraining them by their rival ambitions." In September 1861, former colonial secretary Sir Edward Bulwar-Lytton remarked that a permanent division of the United States would benefit the "safety of Europe." A continental-sized United States, he explained, "hung over Europe like a gathering and destructive thundercloud...[but] as America shall become subdivided into separate states...her ambition would be less formidable for the rest of the world." Dean B. Mahin explains at length in his excellent book, *One War at a Time: The International Dimensions of the American Civil War*, that British sympathy for the Confederacy was based on "geopolitical, political and economic factors."

Napoleon III's France, likewise, desired Confederate independence for similar geopolitical reasons. France had imperial ambitions in Mexico. As Mahin explains, "Napoleon thought an independent Confederacy would provide a buffer between royalist Mexico and the republican United States." France's minister to Washington, Edouard-Henri Mercier, was among the strongest advocates of European intervention on the side of the Confederacy.

Ultimately, skillful diplomacy by the Lincoln Administration combined with important and timely Union military victories convinced the two European powers to refrain from official recognition of the Confederacy and intervention in the war.

The history of the 20th century proved that, in the long term, British and French sympathies during the Civil War were misplaced. Twice during that century, the United States effectively intervened in world wars to help defeat the enemies of Britain and France. During the long Cold War that followed, the United States formally and effectively guaranteed the security of Britain and France against the Soviet geopolitical threat. Had the United States failed to defeat the Confederacy in the Civil War and thereafter shared the center of North America with a strong, hostile power, it is unlikely that it would have had the geopolitical freedom to intervene so effectively in European and Asian affairs during the 20th century. In this geo-historical sense, the defeats of Hitler's Germany, Imperial Japan and the Soviet Union were made possible by the Union victory in the Civil War.

As British historian Brian Holden Reid put it, "It is because the North brought the Civil War to a victorious conclusion and thus prevented the disintegration of the United States into two...competing republics, that the massive spread of American power and culture was able to occur in the twentieth century."

CHAPTER II
World Wars I and II

Churchill and World War I

We are daily reminded by events in the Balkans, Africa, the Middle East and Central Asia that the "new world order" closely resembles the pre-Cold War world. Americans were led to believe that our victory over Soviet communism in the Cold War would usher in a more peaceful world. Political leaders during the 1992 presidential campaign promised a "peace dividend" and focused their rhetoric on domestic issues, largely ignoring the world around them. As a result, the Clinton Administration appears rudderless in the conflict-ridden post-Cold War world.

It is therefore fortuitous that Scribner's has reprinted the one-volume abridgment of Winston Churchill's classic history of the First World War, *The World Crisis*. Originally a four-volume work, the 1931 abridgment is a masterful history of the Great War, its causes, tragedies and consequences, by an author uniquely situated to tell the whole story: the grand strategy of the War Cabinets, the strategy of the General Staffs, as well as the seemingly endless slaughter of the battlefields. Written from the perspectives of a high official of the British War Cabinet (First Lord of the Admiralty and Minister of Munitions), a frontline combatant, and a distinguished historian, Churchill's description of Great Power diplomacy in a multi-polar, anarchic world, and his unforgettable depiction of the gruesome horrors of battle provide valuable lessons and important insights into the formulation and conduct of foreign policy and military strategy.

For far too many Americans, world history consists only of the Cold War and its immediate aftermath. Their world view is shaped almost entirely by the international structure imposed by the U.S.-Soviet rivalry. Now that that structure no longer imposes its discipline on the rest of the world, long-dormant national, religious and ethnic conflicts have flared anew and lesser powers feel freer to wage war to resolve political disputes. The current conflicts raging in the Balkans and Central Asia are the most visible examples of this phenomenon.

Lest we forget, it was just such ethnic and national conflicts in the Balkans that acted as the spark to ignite the First World War. Churchill in *The World Crisis* recounted the step-by-step approach to total war, beginning with Austria-Hungary's formal annexation of Bosnia and Herzegovina and the subsequent Serbian mobilization in 1908, and culminating in the assassination of the Austrian Archduke at Sarajevo and the subsequent Austrian ultimatum to Serbia. In between, of course, was the Agadir crisis of 1911 and Balkan Wars during 1912-1913. "The terrible cruelties and atrocities which had been perpetrated [during the Balkan Wars]," wrote Churchill, "left a river of blood" between the antagonists.

Balkan infighting by itself, however, was not sufficient to cause a world conflagration. Churchill detailed the gradual formation of Great Power alliances, the naval arms race between Germany and Great Britain, and the mobilization plans of the General Staffs which preceded the outbreak of war and all but ensured that if and when war came, it would be a total war, fought not just between armies, navies and air forces, but between whole nations.

At the outset of the war, Churchill was at the Admiralty directing and overseeing the mobilization of the Grand Fleet upon which, ultimately, rested the security of Great Britain and her empire. Churchill well understood the need for Britain to achieve what Mahan termed "command of the sea." Throughout *The World Crisis*, he proudly pointed to the fleet's important, but often unappreciated accomplishments during the war: "the ceaseless stream of troops and supplies to France,… the worldwide trade of Britain proceeding almost without hindrance…, the intricate movement of reinforcements or expeditions escorted across every ocean from every part of the empire," and the "muzzling" of the German High Seas Fleet.

As the fighting on the Continent settled into the stalemate of trench warfare with its attendant slaughter on a scale then unimagined, Churchill sought to use sea power to effect a decisive strategic advantage and, thereby, shorten the war. Churchill devoted sixteen chapters of *The World Crisis* to the Dardanelles or Gallipoli campaign of 1915, his brainchild which was designed to break the deadlock on the Western front. Most historians agree that the plan to force the Dardanelles to drive the Ottoman Empire from the war and link up with the Russians in the East was sound in conception, but sorely lacking in execution. In the event, the Dardanelles failure led to Churchill's dismissal from the War Cabinet, and Allied commanders continued to expend countless lives in unsuccessful attempts to break through the German defenses in 1916 and 1917.

Churchill also championed a technological innovation designed to penetrate and outflank German defenses: the tank. Initially used ineffectively in small numbers and without doctrinal discipline at the Battle of the Somme in 1916, the tank demonstrated its great potential at Cambrai in 1917 where large numbers penetrated the whole German trench system on a six-mile front, resulting in the capture of ten thousand prisoners and two hundred large guns at a relatively low cost in British lives. Tanks could have been used effectively much earlier in the war, in Churchill's view, "if only the Generals had not been content to fight machine-gun bullets with the breasts of gallant men, and think that that was waging war."

Courageous soldiers on both sides and on two huge fronts hurled themselves at barbed-wire, artillery and machine guns at Verdun, Ypres, the Marne, the Somme, Passchendaele, Tannenberg, the Masurian Lakes and less famous places. The human slaughter was immense, yet no strategic advantage was gained. "The noblest nations of Christendom," wrote Churchill, "mingled in murderous confusion." The great nations were "exchanging lives upon a scale at once more frightful than anything that [had] been witnessed before in the world." "[M]onth after month the gallant divisions of heroic human beings were torn to pieces in this terrible rotation."

The terrible slaughter finally ended in November 1918 after Germany's last great offensive failed, and French, British and American troops gradually pushed the exhausted German army toward its frontiers. The Allies were victorious, but as Churchill noted, victory "proved only less ruinous to the victor than the vanquished."

More than sixty years later, we can still learn much from Churchill's riveting history of the Great War: how regional conflicts among minor powers can be transformed into world-wide conflagrations by Great Power meddling, trip-wire mobilization plans, and opposing Great Power alliances; how an island power (such as the United States) needs to maintain even in peacetime the capability to achieve quickly "command of the sea"; how lesser powers must unite in opposition to any power that threatens Eurasian hegemony; how military strategy and doctrine must continually adjust to new weapons technology; how Great Powers engage in a never-ending competition in offensive and defensive forms of warfare; how tactical and strategic maneuver can achieve military victory at less cost than brute force attrition warfare; and how men and nations sometimes have a seemingly limitless capacity to inflict and endure suffering and death on a vast scale.

Woe to the statesman or military leader who ignores or forgets those lessons.

Woodrow Wilson and the First World War

In *To End All Wars: Woodrow Wilson and the Quest for a New World Order*, Thomas J. Knock, an associate professor of history at Southern Methodist University, presents a one-sided, ideological defense of President Wilson's efforts during and after the First World War to persuade the Senate to ratify the Treaty of Versailles and, thereby, commit the United States to joining the League of Nations. Knock's ideological leftism and utopianism pervade the book. Wilson and other supporters of the Treaty and League are praised for their humane, moral vision of a world of peaceful, democratic, disarmed and equal nations, while Treaty opponents such as Henry Cabot Lodge and Theodore Roosevelt are portrayed as dangerous, jingoistic reactionaries.

The book's ideological difficulties are compounded by Knock's failure to present the struggle over the League of Nations in its proper historical context. One would never know from reading Knock's book that the Great War was caused primarily by Germany's quest for continental hegemony, or that the League of Nations was proposed and formed in the midst of the physical break-up of three great empires composed of numerous national, ethnic, and religious groups. The soundness of Wilson's vision and ideas for a "new world order" can only properly be judged when they are placed in the concrete circumstances of time and place. Knock, however, judges them wholly in the abstract.

One would also never know from reading Knock's book what an abysmal failure the League of Nations turned out to be in the 1920s and 1930s. The League did not prevent German and Russian rearmament. It did not prevent German, Italian, and Japanese conquests. It did not prevent the Second World War. The League of Nations was no more effective than the Kellogg-Briand Pact of 1928 by which over sixty nations, including the U.S., pledged to forego using war as an instrument of national policy. Such utopian schemes have always failed because they overlook or ignore the imperfectability of human beings and governments and the vast cultural, political, religious, national, and ethnic differences among people and states.

Knock notes the important, but often neglected, link between domestic politics and foreign policy in the United States. He rightly credits Wilson's vision of a "New Diplomacy" to an alliance of liberal and socialist intellectuals in the U.S. and Britain in the early 1900s. This intellectual alliance included individuals such as Herbert Croly, Walter Lippmann, Charles Trevelyan, Norman Angell, Jane Addams, Max Eastman, Eugene Debs, and John Reed, and journals such as the *Nation*, the *New Republic*, *Masses*, and *Dial*. These "progressive internationalists" were, according to Knock, the crucial base of Wilson's support for the League which Wilson abandoned in a futile effort to gain the support of moderate Republican senators. This abandonment of the "progressive internationalists," and Wilson's failure promptly to educate the American public about the virtues of the League and the "New Diplomacy," coupled with Wilson's failing health in 1919-1920, in Knock's view, sealed the fate of America's participation in the League.

Knock's book ends with a brief leftist critique of the Cold War and such Cold War realists as George F. Kennan, Henry Kissinger, and Ronald Reagan; praise for the Wilsonian vision of former Soviet President Mikhail Gorbachev; and the author's expression of hope that the United Nations may one day fulfill the vision of Wilson and the "progressive internationalists."

Knock's book will be useful to students and scholars who seek an understanding of the intellectual and ideological foundations of Wilson's "New Diplomacy" and the League of Nations. But anyone wishing to read an objective history of the struggle over the League and a realistic assessment of Wilson's vision and ideas in their historical context must go elsewhere.

The War of the World

The optimists among us who believe in the inevitable progress of man, either forget or ignore the fact that the twentieth century was the bloodiest, most destructive century in human history. The century's two world wars resulted in the deaths of at least 60 million people. The Russian Civil War of 1917-21 killed another 5-6 million. Between them, the tyrannical regimes of Hitler, Stalin, and Mao killed at least another 60 million of their own citizens. Many millions more were killed in dozens of other, smaller conflicts.

The British historian Paul Johnson, in his remarkable book *Modern Times*, attributed the twentieth century's huge death toll to the immense growth of organized state power, the decline of traditional religion, and the rise of totalitarian ideologies and gangster-statesmen. In a new book on twentieth century conflicts, another prolific British historian, Niall Ferguson, points to three other causes: "ethnic conflict, economic volatility, and empires in decline."

Like Johnson's *Modern Times*, Ferguson's book, *The War of the World: Twentieth Century Conflict and the Descent of the West*, weaves together economic, military, political, and geopolitical analyses of the major international events of the twentieth century. In 1901, Ferguson notes, multinational European empires dominated an economically-interdependent world, controlling more than half the world's land surface and half of its population. But economic, demographic, ethnic and political factors, especially in Central and Eastern Europe, worked to undermine imperial rule, at the same time that geopolitical factors led to the clash of empires in Europe and Asia.

This highly combustible mix exploded in 1914, resulting in the Great War, which, as Ferguson explains, "changed everything." Globalization ended. "International trade, investment and emigration collapsed...Plans replaced the market; autarky and protection took the place of free trade." Most importantly, writes Ferguson, the "European empires' grip on the world—which had been the political undergirding of globalization—was dealt a profound, if not quite fatal, blow."

The war's battles, which included the use of poison gas and chemical weapons, produced enormous casualties, and ethnic conflict, especially in Central and Eastern Europe, produced savage atrocities and, in the case of Turkish Armenia, genocide. Four multinational empires fell—Austria-Hungary, the Ottoman Empire, Hohenzollern Germany, and Tsarist Russia. The British and French empires, although victorious, suffered economic, physical, and psychological injuries from which they never fully recovered. It would take another, even more destructive, war to hasten their imperial retreat.

French Marshal Ferdinand Foch, commenting in 1919 on the terms of the peace treaty that ended the First World War, stated (as Winston Churchill wrote, "with singular accuracy"), "This is not peace. It is an armistice for twenty years." Even more than the terms of the armistice, however, it was the forces unleashed by the Great War—economic, demographic, political—that produced the cataclysm of the Second World War. Ferguson details the Bolshevik seizure of power in Russia, the Fascist takeover of Italy, the emergence of Hitler and the Nazis in Germany, and the rise of militarism in Japan that preceded the outbreak of war.

Ferguson contends that the Second World War began, not in September 1939 with Hitler's invasion of Poland, but on July 7, 1937, when "full-blown war broke out between China and Japan." Japanese forces occupied much of China's east coast and inflicted savage brutalities upon the Chinese population. Chinese soldiers and civilians were frequently beheaded, burned alive and buried alive. "A few," writes Ferguson, "were hung by their tongues on metal hooks." In the city of Nanking in 1937-38, women and girls were subjected to organized mass rape and murder. Japanese atrocities followed their armies to Southeast Asia, Korea, the Philippines, and wherever the Rising Sun held sway.

While Japanese forces were brutalizing people who they considered their ethnic inferiors in Asia and the Pacific, Hitler's Germany and Stalin's Russia waged war against whole categories of people in Europe, systematically imprisoning and murdering millions based on race, class, and nationality. "This capacity to treat other human beings as members of an inferior and indeed malignant species...," explains Ferguson, "was one of the crucial reasons why twentieth-century conflict was so violent."

Ferguson makes clear, however, that the Western powers in the war crossed moral lines, too, when they deliberately inflicted civilian casualties by massive incendiary bombings of German and Japanese cities. Yet, contrary to many conventional histories of the U.S. and British air campaigns, Ferguson concludes that bombing German cities "inflicted significant damage on the German war effort," and implies that the incendiary bombings of Tokyo and other cities, and atomic bombings of Hiroshima and Nagasaki, shortened the war and likely saved American and Japanese lives by making an invasion of the main Japanese islands unnecessary.

The chief geopolitical beneficiary of the Second World War, Ferguson believes, was the Soviet Union, which ended the war in control of much of eastern and central Europe, and whose communist allies achieved victory in China and elsewhere in Asia. The remaining European empires—mainly France and Britain—surrendered imperial rule in many parts of the world, forcing the United States to fill the strategic vacuum with the policy of "containment." What Ferguson calls the "War of the World" continued in the guise of the Cold War, as the U.S. sought to contain Soviet encroachments in Europe, the Middle East, East and Southeast Asia, and in other parts of the "third world."

The Korean War of 1950-53, writes Ferguson, was the last conflict in which the great empires clashed directly, but the threat of nuclear destruction kept the war limited. After that, he explains, the Cold War "was fought indirectly in new and more remote theatres, where the strategic stakes (though not the human costs) were lower."

Ferguson does not view the fall of the Soviet Empire in 1989-91 as the final triumph of the West. Indeed, like James Burnham in *Suicide of the West* (1964), one of Ferguson's main themes, as evidenced by the subtitle of the book, is that twentieth century history is about the "descent of the West." "A hundred years ago," he writes, "the West ruled the world. After a century of recurrent internecine conflict between the European empires, that is no longer the case." The West's descent is evidenced not only by its imperial retreat, but also by its declining population relative to other civilizations, especially the Islamic world, in the early twenty-first century.

Ferguson's broad, sweeping, and provocative history of twentieth century conflict is a grim reminder that war, terror and strife are part of the human condition. As he warns, "We shall avoid another century of conflict only if we understand the forces that caused the last one—the dark forces that conjure up ethnic conflict and imperial rivalry out of economic crisis, and in doing so negate our common humanity. They are forces that stir within us still."

The Terrible Shadow of the First World War

November 11, 2008, marks the 90th anniversary of the end of one of the most cataclysmic events of human history, the First World War. At 11:00am on November 11, 1918, the guns that had been decimating soldiers for more than four years fell silent. Almost 10 million soldiers lay dead. Large areas of Europe, Asia, and Africa were scarred with craters produced by artillery and mines, and trenches dug by millions of soldiers. In Winston Churchill's memorable words, "All the horrors of all the ages were brought together, and not only armies but whole populations were thrust into the midst of them."[1]

The physical carnage produced by the war, however, paled in comparison to the moral and political carnage that the war created and that shaped the rest of the 20th century. The American diplomat and historian George F. Kennan rightly called the First World War the "seminal catastrophe" of the 20th century. It marked the great divide between the old world and its religious and politically conservative values and customs and the new world, described so perceptively by the British historian Paul Johnson as "a world adrift, having left its moorings in traditional law and morality."[2]

Four old world empires—Hapsburg, Hohenzollern, Romanov, and Ottoman—fell as a result of the First World War. Secular totalitarian ideologies, reminiscent of the Terror of the French Revolution, seized power in Russia, Italy, Japan, and eventually Germany, China and smaller countries. Those secular ideologies produced what Johnson calls "gangster-statesmen" imbued with the "Will to Power" and willing and able to make "human sacrifices to ideology" on an unprecedented and monstrous scale.[3]

In a very real sense, the Armenian genocide, the Russian Civil War, Lenin's "war communism," Stalin's forced collectivization and starvation of the Ukrainian and Russian peasantry, the Great Terror, the Gulag Archipelago, the Nazi Holocaust, the rape of Nanking, the 60 million dead of the Second World War, the Korean and Vietnam Wars, the nuclear arms race, Mao's Great Leap Forward and Cultural Revolution, the Middle East wars and conflict, Pol Pot's Cambodian genocide, and ethnic cleansing in the Balkans are all offspring of the First World War.

The spark that ignited that great conflagration was the assassination in Sarajevo of the heir to the Hapsburg throne by a Serbian terrorist, Gavrilo Princip, on June 28, 1914. The European great powers had for decades been gradually splitting into two alliances on the continent, while Germany and Great Britain engaged in a naval arms race. In 1890, the steady, guiding hand of German Chancellor Otto von Bismarck was removed from the increasingly precarious balance of power. A more aggressive and reckless Kaiser Wilhelm II threatened to upset the balance of power and backed Austria-Hungary's effort to punish Serbia and reclaim its dominance in the Balkans. Russia, invoking its self-appointed role as protector of the Slavs, mobilized in support of Serbia. France mobilized in support of Russia and Great Britain eventually came to the aid of France. Old Europe started its path to suicide.

Germany's war plan to swiftly defeat France then attack the Russians, based on ideas and concepts first formulated by General Alfred von Schlieffen, faltered on the Marne River. The course of the war soon proved that technology had outpaced strategy as generals on both sides sent wave after wave of infantry against entrenched enemy positions armed with machine guns. It was mass slaughter of the attackers, and was repeated time and time again throughout the war. On the first day of the Battle of the Somme, July 1, 1916, the British army suffered more than 60,000 casualties, including about 20,000 dead, but little ground was gained. Similar offensives met similar fates throughout the war.

As Europe lurched toward suicide, the United States was brought into the war as a result of Germany's policy of unrestricted submarine warfare. America's involvement tipped the scales in the Allies' favor. In 1918, a final, initially successful, German offensive was halted. German military leaders, with Allied forces closing in, sued for peace and blamed the politicians for defeat.

The Treaty of Versailles blamed Germany for the war, imposed harsh conditions of peace on the German people and government, but it essentially left Germany intact. When French Marshal Foch heard the terms of the treaty, he remarked with, in Churchill's words, singular accuracy, that "This is not Peace. It is an Armistice for twenty years."[4]

President Woodrow Wilson sought to impose a peace on Europe that would make the world safe for democracy. His utopian vision of a League of Nations clashed with the reality of aggressive totalitarian powers, fueled by secular, universal ideologies, that sought to impose their rule and expand their power as far as their armies and navies would take them. There was no escaping the consequences of the First World War. It shaped everything that came after it. Its shadow remains over us today.

ENDNOTES

1. Winston S. Churchill, *The World Crisis* (New York: Charles Scribner's Sons, 1931), p. 4.

2. Paul Johnson, *Modern Times: The World From the Twenties to the Eighties* (New York: Harper & Row Publishers, 1983), p. 48.

3. *Ibid.* at p. 261.

4. Winston S. Churchill, *The Gathering Storm* (Boston: Houghton Mifflin Company, 1948), p. 7.

Winston Churchill and the Wilderness Years

Winston Churchill is rightly acclaimed for his spirited and inspiring wartime leadership, particularly in 1940-1941, when Britain stood valiantly alone against the terrifying and seemingly unbeatable Nazi onslaught. But his most memorable and courageous acts of public service—his "finest hours"—occurred between 1932 and 1940, when from the depths of the political wilderness he waged a lonely, unpopular, but vigilant struggle to persuade his own countrymen and the other democracies to rearm and to resist Nazi encroachments.

William Manchester's second volume of *The Last Lion: Winston Spencer Churchill, Alone: 1932-1940*, brilliantly recounts Churchill's private and public life during the "wilderness years" of the 1930s when successive British governments complacently ignored his repeated warnings about the Nazi threat and deliberately excluded him from power. Manchester portrays Churchill as a man who greatly desired and vigorously sought after high political office, but who would not compromise with honor and the safety of the British Empire to curry political favor. The same cannot be said about the inept politicians who led Britain toward disaster in the 1930s—Ramsay MacDonald, Stanley Baldwin, John Simon, Nevile Henderson, Horace Wilson, and Neville Chamberlain. In one of history's more tragic ironies, the man best suited to provide the leadership to prevent war was relegated to the role of prophet—a prophet, moreover, who was largely ignored. Churchill's words about Hitler and Nazism fell mostly on deaf ears.

Yet, what powerful words they were. Manchester treats the reader of this volume to numerous excerpts from Churchill's most stirring speeches. For example, when the Third Reich was still in its infancy, Churchill urged rearmament, claiming that "the only choice open is the grim old choice our forefathers had to face, namely, whether we shall be prepared to defend our rights, our liberties, and indeed our lives." Or again, in the wake of Hitler's occupation of the Rhineland, Churchill warned,

> An enormous triumph has been gained by the Nazi regime....The violation of the Rhineland is serious from the point of view of the menace to which it exposes Holland, Belgium, and France. It is also serious from the fact that when fortified...it will be a barrier acrossGermany's front door, which will leave her free to sally out eastward and southward by the back door.

On another occasion, he mercilessly ridiculed the Government's refusal to create a ministry of supply to coordinate defense production, by exclaiming in the House of Commons: "So they go on in strange paradox, decided to be undecided, resolved to be irresolute, adamant for drift, solid for fluidity, all powerful to be impotent. So we go on preparing more months and years—precious, perhaps vital to the greatness of Britain—for the locusts to eat."

And, perhaps most memorably, amid national euphoria over the Munich Agreement, Churchill pleaded that the British people:

> ...should know that there has been gross neglect and deficiency in our defenses; they should know that we have sustained a defeat without a war, the consequences of which will travel far with us along our road; they should know that we have passed an awful milestone in our history, when the whole equilibrium of Europe has been deranged, and that the terrible words have for the time being been pronounced against the Western democracies: "Thou art weighed in the balance and found wanting." And do not suppose that this is the end. This is only the beginning of the reckoning. This is only the first sip—the first foretaste of a bitter cup which will be proffered to us year by year—unless— by a supreme recovery of our moral health and martial vigour, we arise and take our stand for freedom, as in the olden time.

Churchill would speak confidently about the growing Nazi threat because he regularly was provided with confidential information—facts and figures about German rearmament and British military deficiencies—which His Majesty's Government tried to conceal. Indeed, the supporting heroes in Manchester's book are Churchill's unsung and largely unknown allies in the struggle against appeasement who risked their careers to keep Churchill informed: Robert Vansittart, Ralph Wigram, Desmond Morton, Duncan Sandys, Henry Strakosch, John Baker White, A.C. Temperley, Rex Leeper, Michael Creswell and Valentine Lawford. And, of course, there was "the Prof," Frederick Lindemann, Churchill's friend and principal adviser on scientific matters, whose "beautiful brain" (the phrase is Churchill's) in Manchester's judgment was "worth several divisions in the struggle to save England from Adolf Hitler." In this sense, contrary to the subtitle of this volume, Churchill was not alone.

Manchester has an enviable talent for weaving the personal and private lives of his subjects into the larger historical epic, as he demonstrated in his magnificent biography of Douglas MacArthur, *American Caesar*, and in the first volume of *The Last Lion*. Churchill's life at his beloved Chartwell was, in many ways, as interesting and eventful as his public life. He had a deeply loving relationship with his wife Clementine, but a steadily deteriorating one with his son Randolph. He counted among his friends the American financier Bernard Baruch and the comedian Charlie Chaplin, but also the eccentric Professor Lindemann.

At the end of Manchester's second volume, with appeasement completely discredited and France under siege by German panzers, Churchill had at long last attained full power as Prime Minister in a War Cabinet. He later wrote of this moment: "I felt as if I were walking with Destiny, and that all my past life had been but a preparation for this hour and for this trial." He offered his countrymen only "blood, toil, tears and sweat," and focused their attention and efforts on one goal: "victory, victory at all costs, victory in spite of all terror, victory however long and hard the road may be...."

The Immediate Origins of the Second World War

September 1, 1989 marked the fiftieth anniversary of Nazi Germany's invasion of Poland and the beginning of the Second World War. On September 3, 1939, after nearly six years of clinging to the failed policy of appeasement of the European dictators, the governments of Britain and France fulfilled their pledge to Poland by declaring war on Germany. *How War Came* is Donald Cameron Watt's majestic diplomatic history of the twelve months which preceded the outbreak of war— twelve months of mistrust, misapprehensions, misunderstandings and miscalculations on the part of European, Asian, and American diplomats and statesmen.

The euphoria which immediately followed the signing of the Munich Agreement in September 1938—an agreement which British Prime Minister Neville Chamberlain heralded as signifying "peace in our time," but which Winston Churchill, Chamberlain's chief critic in Parliament, denounced as a "defeat without a war" for Czechoslovakia and the Western democracies—soon ebbed with the gradual realization that the incorporation of the Sudetenland into the Nazi Reich failed to satiate Hitler's appetite for territory and power. During the next year, the diplomats of the world's great and lesser powers engaged in a frenzied, but ultimately fruitless, effort to prevent the outbreak of armed conflict.

The main participants in this diplomatic drama were the statesmen and diplomats of Germany, Britain, France, the Soviet Union, Italy, and Poland. The first four countries were great powers. Italy's importance derived from her alliance with Germany and Mussolini's personal relationship with Hitler, while Poland's significance lay in the unfortunate fact that she was the immediate object of Hitler's territorial ambitions and thereby the focus of much of the diplomatic activity of 1939.

Italy's foreign policy was conducted by Mussolini and his son-in-law Count Ciano, the foreign minister. Both men gloried in the role of world statesmen which Italy's alliance with Germany allowed them to play. But neither man, particularly Ciano, was anxious to fight a general European war. In fact, Ciano launched a last ditch effort in August 1939 to persuade Hitler to refrain from attacking Poland. At one meeting, Ciano asked German Foreign Minister Joachim von Ribbentrop, "Is it only Danzig that you want?" Von Ribbentrop replied, "We want much more than that. We want war."

Foreign Minister Jozef Beck dominated Poland's pre-war foreign policy. Watt describes Beck as "devouringly ambitious and arrogantly unrealistic in his judgment of the strength of Poland's international position." Beck, influenced by post-World War I geopolitical writings, sought to create "a great bloc of powers under Polish leadership stretching from Scandinavia to the Adriatic as a permanent entity between Germany and the Soviet Union." Indeed, the great geopolitical theorist Halford J. Mackinder had proposed such an arrangement in his seminal work, *Democratic Ideals and Reality* in 1919. But Beck's "great bloc of powers" never materialized and he underestimated, along with most European statesmen, the value of an alliance with Soviet Russia against Germany.

Soviet foreign policy during this period shifted from attempts at reaching collective security arrangements with the Western powers and East European states against Germany to the signing of a non-aggression pact with Germany in August 1939 which included a secret clause that carved most of Central and Eastern Europe into German and Soviet spheres of influence. The Western democracies, as a result of Stalin's massive purge of his military forces, largely dismissed the Soviets as a major player on the European chessboard. Stalin, for his part, feared that British and French diplomacy was aimed at diverting Hitler's ambition eastward. With the signing of the non-aggression pact, Stalin became Hitler's accomplice in engulfing the world in another war, and for this his country paid a terrible price two years later when Hitler launched "Operation Barbarossa," the invasion of the Soviet Union.

On paper, France had the strongest army in Europe, but her military leaders were wedded to outdated strategic and tactical concepts, while her political leaders could not escape from the memories of the horrible slaughters at Verdun, the Marne, Ypres, and the Somme. The French Cabinet, led by Daladier and Bonnet, was hopelessly divided, indecisive, and all too willing to follow Neville Chamberlain's lead. France, more so than Britain, favored an alliance with the Soviet Union, but her penchant for waiting on events led, ultimately, to events overtaking her. The politically fragile Third Republic was soon to be crushed by German stukas and panzers.

Watt rightly judges Chamberlain and Hitler to have been the most important individuals in the events of 1939. Chamberlain's desire for peace overrode his sensible dislike of Hitler and the Nazis, while his virulent anti-Bolshevism clouded his judgment as to the value of a British-Soviet alliance against Germany. Gradually, as Hitler's aggressive intentions became unmistakably clear,Chamberlain accepted the advice of his foreign minister, Lord Halifax, and bowed to public opinion by committing Britain to the defense of Poland. Alas, this was a commitment which, given the previous record of appeasement, would not deter the German dictator.

Watt also details the efforts to avert war undertaken by President Roosevelt, Pope Pius XII, and several amateur diplomats. But despite the efforts of all these statesmen and diplomats, professional and amateur alike, war came. Why? Watt's answer is simple, yet unnerving: war came because Hitler wanted war. As Watt writes: "What is so extraordinary in the events which led to the outbreak of the Second World War is that Hitler's will for war was able to overcome the reluctance with which everybody else approached it." Watt believes that the only people who could have stopped Hitler permanently and prevented war were the German generals and soldiers who opposed Hitler's rule.

The "lessons" of history are often overdrawn, but today's diplomats and political leaders should ponder the fundamental lessons of *How War Came*: war is not caused by misunderstandings among nations or the interplay of impersonal forces; war is a willed political act.

Allied Strategy and Tactics in the Second World War

Two major themes pervade John Ellis' book on Allied tactics and strategy in the Second World War. First, Allied economic and material preponderance made inevitable the defeat of Nazi Germany, Italy and Japan in a protracted, total war. Second, British, American, and Soviet commanders used this economic and material preponderance to wage a war of attrition on land, at sea, and in the air, relying on "brute force" rather then strategy. As a consequence, according to Ellis, the Allied victory came at greater cost in resources and lives than was necessary.

Ellis relies on statistical data and information on the relative quantity, quality, and characteristics of weapons to demonstrate the massive Allied material superiority in the Second World War. In addition to providing a 23-page statistical appendix, Ellis neatly weaves statistical information throughout the text. Ellis is very adept at handling and making sense out of a vast array of information. Weapons production statistics are carefully qualified by distinctions in quality and difficulties encountered in supplying forces on the battlefields. Given all those important distinctions and qualifications, however, the numerical disparities between Allied and Axis forces in all theaters of war, and in all aspects of warfare, are telling. In the last two years of the war on the eastern front, the Soviets attained advantages over Germany of over three-to-one in combat aircraft, four-to-one in artillery, and over five-to-one in armored fighting vehicles. In North Africa by October 1942, the Allies achieved a four-to-one advantage in tanks and combat aircraft, a twelve-to-one advantage in artillery, and a nearly thirty-to-one advantage in anti-tank weapons over German and Italian forces. In Italy by 1945, the allies gained a two-to-one superiority in medium guns, a five-to-one lead in heavy guns, nearly a ten-to-one advantage in tanks, and more than a ten-to-one advantage in combat aircraft. In Northwest Europe, the Allies achieved better than a five-to-one advantage in tanks and more than a twenty-to-one advantage in combat aircraft by 1945. Finally, in the Pacific by 1945, the U.S. achieved over Japan a four-to-one lead in front-line aircraft, a five-to-one advantage in battleships, a seven-to-one advantage in aircraft carriers and destroyers, and better than a thirty-to-one lead in escort carriers.

While he marvels at Allied industrial capabilities, Ellis is far less complimentary of the tactics employed by Allied field commanders. Ellis in fact has very little good to say about *any* Allied commander. He is most critical of Air Marshal Arthur Harris who formulated and implemented, in Ellis's terms, the militarily and morally dubious policy of urban area saturation bombing, and filed Marshal Bernard Montgomery, whose boundless caution kept him from even attempting tactical maneuvers which might have shortened the war in North Africa and Northwest Europe. American commanders fare little better: Ellis calls Patton "one of the best traffic policemen in the history of warfare," and argues that "he was not a particularly successful combat commander."

Compare that to British Major-General H. Essame's conclusion that Patton should join Murat, Sherman, Stonewall Jackson, Manstein and Rommel on the list of great battlefield commanders; or to German Field Marshal von Rundstedt's comment to the historian B.H. Liddell Hart that Patton and Montgomery "were the two best" Allied commanders during the war. Soviet commanders, too, are criticized for failing "to effect or exploit strategic penetrations by free-ranging mobile forces," and instead relying on "mass frontal attacks" which produced "appalling casualties" among their own troops.

It is surely the military historian's responsibility to use statistics and hindsight to critically assess the actions of battlefield commanders, but this frequently leads to a degree of certainty forty years later on the historian's part which was unavailable to commanders during the heat of battle. In this respect, Ellis could use a dose of humility.

The author's analysis of Allied tactics in World War II would have been more complete if he had discussed the institutional rejection by Allied military bureaucracies of armored warfare doctrines propounded by J.F.C. Fuller and B.H. Liddell Hart prior to the outbreak of war. Those doctrines, unfortunately, found more fertile ground in Germany where commanders like Heinz Guderian and Erwin Rommel put them to good use in the early phases of the war. A nation's military commanders are products of the cultures and institutions that influence and train them.

But these are minor quibbles with what is otherwise an outstanding work of military history. Like all good historians, Ellis concludes with a cautionary note intended for current leaders: "Unless our histories take full cognizance of just how big a margin was required [to win] the Second World War, we shall leave ourselves without adequate conventional capacity in any future war."

Somewhere in France, Somewhere in Germany

Sixty-four years ago, on June 6, 1944, my father, Frank F. Sempa, was one of thousands of American soldiers on ships in the English Channel waiting his turn to land on Omaha Beach on France's Normandy coast to participate in the historic invasion of Hitler's fortress Europe. At the time, he was a Sergeant in the 29th Division's 175th infantry regiment that was part of V Corps which was assigned to reinforce and exploit whatever beachhead had been gained at great cost by the initial D-Day assaults made by the 1st Division and the 116th infantry regiment of the 29th Division. My father's regiment landed on Omaha Beach on June 7, D-Day +1.

For the next eleven months, my father and his regiment and division fought its way across France and into Germany, reaching the Elbe River by V-E Day, May 8, 1945. There have been several fine accounts written of the 29th Division's historic journey from D-Day to the end of the war, including Joseph Ewing's *29 Let's Go*, Joseph Balkoski's *Beyond the Beachhead*, Michael Reynolds' *Eagles and Bulldogs in Normandy 1944*, Leo Daugherty's *The Battle of the Hedgerows*, and John McManus' *The Americans at Normandy*. In this article, I will draw on those books and others, but also from the snippets of history gleaned from the numerous letters that my father wrote during the war to his parents (my grandparents) from "Somewhere in France" and "Somewhere in Germany," an interview he did, shortly after returning home from the war, with the local newspaper, the *Scranton Tribune*, where he worked for more than forty years as a reporter and editor, an article he wrote for that paper on the 25th anniversary of the D-Day landings, and my own recollections of the few times that he would talk about some of his war experiences.

Frank F. Sempa was drafted into the army at the age of 24 on April 25, 1941. At the time, he lived with his parents and two brothers in Avoca, a small town in northeastern Pennsylvania, and worked as a local correspondent for the *Scranton Tribune*. He subsequently trained at Ft. George G. Meade in Maryland and other forts in Virginia, the Carolinas, and Florida. In October 1942, he and his regiment traveled from New Jersey across the Atlantic on the *Queen Elizabeth* to Scotland, settling at the old British Army cavalry camp at Tidworth Barracks near Andover and Salisbury. There and at other locations in Great Britain, the 29th Division trained for the long-planned opening of the second front in Europe.

The decision as to where and when to open the second front in Europe was repeatedly debated by President Franklin Roosevelt, Prime Minister Winston Churchill and their top advisers. Soviet dictator Josef Stalin, whose Russian troops bore the brunt of the fighting in Europe during the first few years of the war, continuously urged the Western leaders to open a second front in Western Europe. The cross-channel invasion had been planned and postponed in earlier years, largely at the urging of Churchill who instead advocated the allied moves into North Africa, Sicily, and Italy. By the spring of 1944, however, the die was cast. General Dwight D. Eisenhower, appointed supreme commander of the cross-channel invasion, decided that D-Day would be in early June.

On D-Day, my father and the other soldiers of the 175th regiment boarded ships at Falmouth and sailed into the rough waters of the English Channel. I recall him telling me how rough the sea was that day, and later how difficult it was to climb down the rope ladders onto the landing craft on the approach to Omaha Beach. It was a lot rougher that day, however, for the American troops who made the initial landings in the face of murderous German machine-gun and artillery fire. Those brave troops suffered tremendous casualties in their effort to establish a secure beachhead. I remember my father telling me later that most of the war's real heroes never came back; they are buried, he said, under those Crosses and Stars of David at the American Cemetery in Normandy and elsewhere in Europe and the Pacific.

At 11:46 am on June 7, 1944, General Charles Gerhardt ordered Col. Paul Goode, commander of the 175th, to begin landing my father's regiment on Omaha Beach. "[N]avy motorboats buzzed around the transport ships, as crewman…shouted over loudspeakers, 'All elements of the One-seventy-fifth Infantry urgently needed on the beach.'"[1] As my father and his regiment hit the beach, they were under intermittent machine-gun, sniper, and artillery fire. At least two landing crafts struck mines on their way to the beach. Captain Robert M. Miller later commented that the beach "looked like something out of Dante's Inferno."[2] The men of the 175th saw the bodies of the American soldiers that were killed the previous day, and many of them were wearing the blue and gray patch of the 29th Division. My father later wrote, "Death was everywhere on Omaha Beach."[3]

The 175th landed at the Les Moulins draw, about a mile east of where they were supposed to land. Amidst confusion and the "fog of war," they were ordered to move west and advance inland near the Vierville draw and take the town of Isigny, located at the confluence of the Vire and Aure Rivers. In two days of fighting, the 175th captured Isigny which served two strategic purposes: first, it enabled the entire 29th Division to advance even though the Germans had flooded the Aure River valley; and second, it facilitated the junction of the Omaha and Utah Beachheads.[4] British military historian Michael Reynolds called the capture of Isigny by the 175th "a remarkable achievement." "In less than the thirty-six hours after coming ashore on OMAHA beach," Reynolds explained, "Colonel Paul Goode's Regiment had advanced 20km and eliminated the German corridor between the OMAHA and UTAH beachheads. In the face of this rapid advance, the entire enemy defensive system north of the Aure valley…collapsed. And the whole operation had been achieved on foot—and with little or no sleep or food."[5]

Six days after landing on Omaha Beach, and four days after the capture of Isigny, my father wrote his first letters from France. He told his brother John that he "was now inside the Fortress of Europe," and was writing from his foxhole which he described as his new home. "Have had plenty of experiences to date," he wrote, "but they will have to wait until later…Can't write too much as Censorship will not permit it until a later date." In a separate letter to his parents the same day, my father wrote that he had experienced "plenty of excitement," and noted that his home was a foxhole.[6]

Three days later on June 16, my father's regiment began its attack toward St. Lo, and for two days it steadily advanced. But this was hedgerow country and the Germans began to counterattack. "The fighting," one historian wrote, "was sickening and desperate."[7] By June 18, the 29th Division was only five miles from St. Lo, but due to stiffening German resistance and the difficulties of hedgerow fighting, St. Lo would not be captured for another month "and only then at a cost of some of the most intense and deadly fighting of the war."[8]

The great British military historian John Keegan has explained that the hedgerows in Normandy were "field boundaries planted by...Celtic farmers 2000 years earlier. Over two millennia their entangled roots had collected earth to form banks as much as ten feet thick." "To the Germans," Keegan wrote, "they offered almost impregnable defensive lines at intervals of 100 or 200 yards. To the attacking American infantry they were death traps."[9] One American General wrote of the hedgerow fighting:

> I doubt if anyone who ever ducked bullets and shells in the hedgerows waded through the mud on foot, and scrambled over the hedgerows never knowing when he might find himself looking into the muzzle of a German tank gun, will look back on those days with any remembered feeling other than of the deadly un- relenting fatigue and danger. Except when the Germans counter- attacked, there was so little result to show for so much suffering; just a few hedgerows gained, each one just like those already behind and those still to take.[10]

"Whenever the 29ers stormed and won a hedgerow," writes Balkoski, "there always seemed to be another one 100 yards behind it resolutely defended by the enemy."[11]

Writing from hedgerow country on June 18 and 19, my father remarked to his parents, "Whoever said 'war is hell' was right... If I told you of some of my experiences you'd probably worry so I just won't." In early July as the campaign to take St. Lo continued, my father noted in a letter that he'd been trying to write more letters, but "everytime I start the shells start thick and fast and I have to give up." He expressed the hope that "it lets up a bit," and said he was "a bit tired after being in the front lines for almost 40 days."

On July 18, 1944, elements of the 29th, 35th, 30th, and 2nd Divisions, assisted by the 3rd Armored Division, captured the rubble of St.Lo. That day, from the outskirts of the town, my father wrote, "War is hell so why talk about it." The capture of St.Lo and its immediate aftermath "marked the first time in forty-five days that the 29th as a division had been out of contact with the enemy. Since the

Omaha Beach landings, [the 29th] had been in front every day of the long six-week campaign." The battle for St.Lo was "the most costly engagement in the history of the Division."[12] Three days after the fall of St.Lo, my father told his parents that he was finally "enjoying a bit of a rest—after days of continuous action."

June and July 1944 were the costliest months of the war for the 175th regiment and the 29th Division as a whole. In those two months, the 175th suffered more than 2,300 casualties (dead, wounded, missing), while the 29th Division as a whole suffered over 8,600 casualties. The costly Normandy campaign, however, set the stage for the launching of Operation COBRA, a concentrated armored dash across France conceived by General Omar Bradley and executed by, among others, General George S. Patton's troops.

My father and other infantrymen in Europe were, of course, oblivious to the high policy and diplomatic discussions among the allied war leaders and their advisers. FDR and Churchill debated, sometimes heatedly, the political and military issues involved in the plans to militarily defeat Germany and Italy and bring the war to a successful political conclusion. The war's end seemed within reach in the late summer of 1944.

In early August 1944, "highly encouraging war bulletins tended to bolster the morale" of U.S. soldiers. "The thrill of victory had taken possession of the troops."[13] This was reflected in my father's letters during that time. On August 8, my father wrote to his parents that the "war news is mighty good and its just a matter of a short time and then it will be all over." Later that month, he speculated in a letter that he might be home for Christmas.

In late August 1944, Paris was liberated. The circumstances under which Paris was liberated involved much diplomatic wrangling and maneuvering, especially among the contending leaders of the Free French movement; another example of diplomacy guiding military decisions. As Paris was being liberated, my father's regiment and division were participating in the campaign to take Brest, the second largest port in France and home to a German submarine base. During that campaign, the 175th engaged in an eight-day battle for "Hill 103," the commanding position in the area, and a five-day battle for the city of Brest which was taken on September 18, 1944. In an October 7 letter, my father revealed to his parents that he participated in the Brest campaign, and that he had been in Paris, Belgium and Holland. It was also in that same October 7 letter that my father revealed that he was now "somewhere in Germany."

Also on October 7, 1944, Lt. Col. William C. Purnell recommended to the 29th Division's commanding general that my father be appointed a temporary warrant officer. The recommendation noted that Sgt. Sempa's character was "Excellent," and stated further that "Sgt. Sempa has at all times demonstrated superior leadership, courage and performed his duties in a superior manner."

In early November 1944, Franklin D. Roosevelt was elected to an unprecedented fourth term as President and Commander-in-Chief of the armed services. On November 9, my father wrote that FDR's election "bore out my prediction that a change at this time was uncalled for," and in a subsequent letter he told his parents that he voted for FDR.

In mid-November, the 175th began a move toward Julich. During this campaign, my father's regiment participated in attacks on Siersdorf, Bettendorf, Aldenhoven, Niedermerz, and Bourheim. By December, the 29th Division stood across the Ruhr River from Julich, but the crossing of the Ruhr was delayed for almost three months by the German counteroffensive in the Ardennes Forest, known to history as the Battle of the Bulge.

In a moving letter dated December 3, 1944 from "Somewhere in Germany," my father informed his parents that he had seen his brother Eddie (my Uncle Eddie), who was fighting with another unit nearby:

> Dear Mom and Dad:
> Got some good news for you today. Saw Eddie and let me tell You he looks swell. Found out his whereabouts this morning. Permission to go was gladly given and a jeep furnished.... He was tickled pink to see me. Spent about 3 hours with him. Talked about most everything under the sun....
>
> Love, Frankie

It was also in December that my father informed his parents that he had been promoted to Tech Sergeant, and was awarded the prestigious Combat Infantryman's Badge.

On Christmas Eve, 1944, my father wrote two letters to his parents. He mentioned decorating a Christmas tree, and noted that the "surroundings aren't the best here in war torn Germany but we are making the best of it." "Tomorrow," he wrote, "is just another day in this war but that certain something will be there in everyone's heart." He also urged his parents to be "thankful that we are all alive—even though not together," and commented that "for certain we will all be together by next Xmas."

After a relatively quiet holiday, however, it was back to the war. In January 1945, the Russians began an offensive that would ultimately lead them to Berlin. On January 17, my father informed his parents that "News from the Russian front today is good and very likely to hasten the end of this war." In late February, Julich fell to the 29th Division, and in early March my father's regiment took part in the capture of Munchen-Gladbach.[14]

On March 9, 1945, my father was awarded a Bronze Star. The citation accompanying the medal reads as follows:

> T Sgt Frank F Sempa, 33024465, (then S Sgt and T Sgt), 175th Inf, U S Army, for meritorious Service in military operations against the enemy in Western Europe. From 7 June 1944 to 13 February 1945, T Sgt Sempa, Communications Sergeant, excelled in the performance of his duties and contributed materially to the fine record established by the organization of which he is a member. The high standards of

courage, initiative and discipline required during long periods of combat were met by T Sgt Sempa in a manner that reflect great credit upon himself and the Military Service. Entered Military Service from Pennsylvania.

In late March-early April, the 29th Division crossed the Rhine River and headed toward the Elbe River. On April 12, 1945, President Roosevelt died in Warm Springs, Georgia. The next day, my father wrote to his parents that "News of FDR's death came as a distinct shock to all of us here. It's a shame he didn't live to see the victory he fought so hard for..."

On May 2, 1945, a German V-2 Rocket Division surrendered to the 175th. The war in Europe was coming to an end. As the American troops moved farther into Germany, Nazi concentration camps and slave-labor camps were liberated. In a letter dated May 5, 1945, my father mentioned to his parents that he saw a slave-labor camp. "Everything you read about those German camps is true," he wrote. "I saw one of them and let me tell you it was brutal...You should have seen this camp. Very, very brutal. Can't understand how anybody could treat people like the Germans treated the slave laborers."

Two days later, my father informed his parents that, "The radio just informed us that tomorrow, 8 May, will be V-E Day. That's the day we have been waiting for.... Guess I'll go and get drunk tomorrow. It sure is worth a celebration. It sure has been a long and hard struggle."

On May 25, 1945, my father was promoted to Master Sergeant. Soldiers were demobilized according to a point system and needed 84 points to be discharged. My father had 110 points. He was separated from the service on July 9, 1945. During his service, he earned the Bronze Star, the Combat Infantryman's Badge, the Arrowhead for the assault on Omaha Beach, four major engagement stars, five overseas stripes, and the Good Conduct Ribbon. He returned to his job as a reporter and later city editor for the *Scranton Tribune*. He died in 1988.

Like many of his generation, he rarely spoke about his wartime experiences. He considered himself very fortunate to have survived the war unscathed, and he always taught me to honor those who made the supreme sacrifice for our country.

ENDNOTES

1. John C. McManus, *The Americans at Normandy: The Summer of 1944—The American War From the Normandy Beaches to Falaise* (New York: Forge, 2004), p. 36.

2. Joseph Balkoski, *Beyond the Beachhead: The 29th Infantry Division in Normandy* (Mechanicsburg, PA: Stackpole Books, 1999), p. 152.

3. *Scranton Tribune*, June 6, 1969.

4. Joseph Ewing, *29 Let's Go: A History of the 29th Infantry Division in World War II* (Washington, D.C.: Infantry Journal Press, 1948), p. 62.

5. Michael Reynolds, *Eagles and Bulldogs in Normandy 1944* (Havertown, PA: Casemate, 2003), p. 124.

6. My grandmother kept my father's letters from France and Germany in a shoebox in our family's home in Avoca. Many years ago, after my father's death in 1988, I happened upon them in the cellar of the home. They have since been donated to the Army War College in Carlisle, Pennsylvania.

7. McManus, *The Americans at Normandy*, p. 133.

8. Leo Daugherty, *The Battle of the Hedgerows: Bradley's First Army in Normandy, June-July 1944* (London: Brown Partworks Limited, 2001), pp. 89-90.

9. John Keegan, *The Second World War* (New York: Viking, 1989), p. 390.

10. *St. Lo* (Washington, D.C.: Historical Division, War Department, 1946), p. 125.

11. Balkoski, *Beyond the Beachhead*, p. 190.

12. Ewing, *29 Let's Go*, p. 104.

13. Ewing, *29 Let's Go*, p. 120.

14. Ewing, *29 Let's Go*, p. 243.

CHAPTER III
The Cold War

This War Called Peace

It is refreshing to read a book about East-West relations wherein the authors dispense with the mindless clichés so familiar to this genre. In nearly 300 pages, there are no allusions to "creating a favorable climate for easing tensions," or "managing U.S.-Soviet competition," or "creating incentives to modify Soviet behavior," etc., etc. The authors eschew the language of détente. In fact, the book amounts to an indictment of détente. Brian Crozier, Drew Middleton and Jeremy Murray-Brown, like a skilled team of prosecutors, marshal an overwhelming mass of evidence in pressing this indictment.

The book's message is blunt and discomforting: the West is on the receiving end of a war with the Soviet Union, but few in the West are conscious of this ongoing conflict.

"This war called peace" was declared in 1919 when Lenin established the Comintern as the instrument of world revolution. Lenin's dream of a communized world, however, could not begin to be fulfilled until the latter part of the Second World War. Specifically, the first "shots" of "this war called peace" were fired in April 1944, when communists led a mutiny in the Greek Navy at Alexandria's harbor. This event signified the beginning of a strategy that would manifest itself in Yugoslavia, China and other countries where communist resistance forces turned upon their ostensible allies in order to improve their postwar political position.

It is worth noting parenthetically that this reference to the Greek mutiny as the beginning of "this war called peace" is undoubtedly attributable to Brian Crozier. It was Crozier's predecessor in the pages of *National Review*, James Burnham, who originally identified this incident as the beginning of what he called the "Third World War" in his 1947 landmark work, *The Struggle for the World*.

The Western leaders in 1944 failed to grasp the significance of the mutiny. It is true that Churchill moved to crush the uprising with commendable speed, but he and Roosevelt continued to underestimate Stalin's intentions. The authors, in fact, offer little in the way of positive assessments of Roosevelt or Churchill during the latter phase of the war.

The surprise here is with regard to Churchill. It has been generally accepted that, while Stalin successfully deceived and out-maneuvered Roosevelt,

Churchill was consistent in his distrust of the Soviet dictator all along. That may be so. Yet, the authors point out that, prior to his famous 1946 "Iron Curtain" speech in Fulton, Missouri (when he was no longer in power), Churchill had not publicly sounded any alarm about the Soviet threat. Indeed, the authors demonstrate how Churchill had busied himself in striking deals with Stalin to divide Rumania, Greece and Yugoslavia—and how, along with FDR, he became an accessory to some of Stalin's transgressions, either by remaining silent (Katyn Forrest Massacre) or actually aiding and abetting (the forcible repatriation of Russians and Cossacks to the USSR). The evidence is persuasive that Churchill's "finest hours" were prior to and in the early years of the Second World War.

The few encomiums bestowed upon Western statesmen are chiefly limited to the men most responsible for formulating and implementing the policy of containment: Truman, Acheson, Marshall, Kennan, McCloy, etc. Those men helped reverse the long-standing U.S. policy of avoiding alliances in peacetime.

Today, Americans take for granted such compacts as NATO and the U.S.-Japanese alliance. It was not always so. Of course, Truman and his advisers, in prodding a shift in American popular attitudes, were helped by Stalin's blundering diplomacy. Americans wanted nothing more than to sustain the "friendly alliance" with the Soviet Union which had been painted in such glowing—indeed, heroic—colors by wartime American propaganda. It is quite possible that, had Stalin acted more patiently—had he maintained the facades of peace and democratic principles a little while longer—America's military and psychological demobilization could have progressed beyond the point of effective return. In the event, the rapid sequence of Soviet actions—in Eastern and Central Europe, in Iran, in the Mediterranean and, finally, in the direct confrontation of the Berlin Blockade—raised an unmistakable specter to which even a war-weary populace could respond, and America accepted the challenge of leading the Free World.

The authors make clear that "this war called peace" has continued unabated. After a brief—in historical terms—period of relative "containment," the Soviet advance resumed in earnest under the tenure of Leonid Brezhnev. Under his rule, "the size and power of the Soviet Empire…expanded enormously, and the goal of victory in the Cold War was no longer a strain on the imagination." Those years witnessed the full satellization of Cuba and the incorporation into the Soviet camp of a growing list of countries: Vietnam, Laos, Cambodia, Angola, South Yemen, Ethiopia, Mozambique, Nicaragua and Afghanistan. The United States suffered a disastrous defeat in Vietnam, followed by a period of national self-emasculation in military and intelligence capabilities, as well as by such setbacks as the loss of a key strategic ally in Iran, the full consequences of which have yet to unfold.

Most significant, however, was the dramatic shift in the military balance of power in favor of the Soviets. Already out-gunned in conventional forces, by the early to mid-1970s America lost her superiority in nuclear forces as well. Henry Kissinger later commented that "rarely in history has a nation so passively accepted such a radical change in the military balance." Reflecting on those events, one is tempted to agree with Solzhenitsyn's observation that "the security of the West today is solely dependent upon the unforeseen Sino-Soviet rift."

Anyone who reads *This War Called Peace* can more soberly assess the significance of the summit meeting in Geneva in the mid 1980s. Consider the following record of such meetings: The summits at Yalta and Potsdam were followed by the extension of Soviet political control over Eastern and most of Central Europe, Soviet pressures on Iran, Greece and Turkey, and the Korean War. The 1955 Geneva Summit was followed by the crushing of the Hungarian rebellion and new crisis over Berlin. The 1961 Vienna meeting preceded the erection of the Berlin Wall, the Cuban missile crisis and the Vietnam War.

After the Glassboro summit came the Soviet invasion of Czechoslovakia. The series of summits in the early and mid-1970s were the background for intensified Soviet involvement in the Middle East, the North Vietnamese conquest of Indochina, and Soviet-inspired and/or supported revolutions in Angola, South Yemen, Ethiopia, Mozambique, Afghanistan and Nicaragua. The Carter-Brezhnev summit was followed by the Soviet invasion of Afghanistan and an accelerated and expanded Soviet conflict strategy in the Central American/Caribbean Sea region.

This is not intended to adduce necessarily a cause-and-effect relationship between the summits and the events that followed. It does suggest, however, that at the very least the summits did not prevent those events from occurring. After each summit, the East-West rivalry continued and, in many cases, intensified. The much-heralded period of détente in the 1970s issued not from effective summitry, but from America's unwillingness to respond effectively to Soviet or Soviet-inspired aggression in many parts of the world. During this period, Soviet policy did not change; ours did.

Prior to the Geneva summit of the mid-1980s, news analysis and commentary noted real "differences" between the superpowers, but emphasized the view that the summit provided a "historic opportunity" to improve U.S.-Soviet relations. Post-summit analysis generally conceded that nothing of substance was accomplished; nevertheless, many commentators opined that the summit created a favorable "atmosphere" for "easing tensions." The *New York Times* proclaimed a new "Spirit of Geneva." Even the Reagan Administration, including the President himself, encouraged the notion that a "fresh start" was made in U.S.-Soviet relations.

Lost in all these expressions of hope is the fact, iterated by Crozier, et al.,that we are at war. As Irving Kristol pointed out in *The National Interest*, this war is fundamentally ideological in nature, and a permanent modus vivendi between the United States and Soviet Union is not possible until one or the other system changes. It is this aspect of the East-West conflict that has persistently eluded the intellectual grasp of so many American elites who continue their obsessive search for chimerical negotiated solutions, deals or settlements that fall somewhere between victory and defeat. As Midge Decter explained in the 40th Anniversary issue of *Commentary*, they fail to understand that for Soviet communism and the West there is no "third way":

> What we have not done…is face up to the fact that Communism is an either/or proposition. Which is to say that Communism is in its nature a revolutionary principle. Which is to say further that in the long run, either Communism in some variant or Western-style democracy in some variant must prevail. It is a case of "them or us." The Soviets see the world this way; it is the source of their renowned patience. They have a policy—they seek to do us in —which is why they can advance, retreat, get tough, act friendly, shift alliances, or whatever else seems to serve their ultimate ends at any particular moment.

This, too, is the message of *This War Called Peace*: the East-West conflict will continue until one or the other system prevails. The 1985 rerun of the "spirit of Geneva" has changed nothing.

James Burnham and the Struggle for the World

Daniel Kelly, a former Foreign Service officer and retired professor of modern European history at New York University and the City University of New York, has written the first full-scale biography of one of the most interesting and important intellectuals of the twentieth century. Between 1932 and 1955, James Burnham traveled the intellectual odyssey from Marxism (the Trotskyite version) to conservatism. But, as Kelly explains in *James Burnham and the Struggle for the World: A Life*, Burnham, throughout this journey and during the rest of his intellectual career, defied precise ideological definition. His views and positions on political issues changed whenever he believed that the empirical evidence justified such change. Though often accused of being an "ideologue," Burnham instead consistently rejected any approach to the study of politics that subordinated empiricism to ideology.

Burnham was born in 1905 into a well-to-do Catholic family in Chicago. His father, an immigrant from England, was a railroad executive. Burnham attended Princeton University where he studied philosophy and graduated first in his class in 1927. After completing post-graduate work in England, he took a position in the philosophy department of New York University, where he became friendly with Philip Wheelwright and Sidney Hook, both of whom had a significant impact on Burnham's early intellectual development. Burnham and Wheelwright founded and edited a literary journal called the *Symposium*. The deepening of the Great Depression in the early 1930s coupled with Burnham's immersion in the works of Marx, Engels, and Leon Trotsky, among others, persuaded him that Marxism provided the best answers and potential solutions to the sufferings of the industrial world.

Gradually, Burnham became a leading member of the Trotskyite wing of the international communist movement. He became a regular contributor to the Marxist journal, the *New International*, where he used his literary skills to defend Trotsky and to call for a socialist revolution in America. However, facts kept getting in the way of ideology. Marx's theories did not fare well when subjected to Burnham's rigorous empirical analyses. He began openly feuding with Trotsky in the mid-to-late 1930s, and ended his ties to the communist movement forever after the signing of the Nazi-Soviet non-aggression pact in August 1939.

It was also during the mid-to-late 1930s that Burnham developed his theory of the "managerial revolution," which became the subject of his first major book on world politics. Kelly's discussion of *The Managerial Revolution*, published to much acclaim in 1941, focuses on the sociopolitical aspects of Burnham's theory, namely that the world's industrial countries were moving toward rule by "managers" rather than capitalists or communists. But *The Managerial Revolution* was also Burnham's first foray into global geopolitics, a subject that

Burnham would repeatedly return to throughout the rest of his intellectual career.

Burnham followed-up the success of *The Managerial Revolution* with the less commercially successful *The Machiavellians* in 1943. Kelly agrees with others who have studied Burnham's writings that *The Machiavellians* contains the intellectual foundation for Burnham's political thought. Borrowing concepts and theories from Machiavelli, Gaetano Mosca, Vilfredo Pareto, Georges Sorel, and Robert Michels, Burnham set forth his own "science of politics," which he used to analyze political events, theories, and rhetoric. He once remarked, notes Kelly, that "the Machiavellians" taught him that "only by renouncing all ideology can we begin to see the world and man."

During the latter part of the Second World War, Burnham worked for the Office of Strategic Services (OSS), the wartime predecessor of the Central Intelligence Agency. In the spring of 1944, he wrote a remarkable and prophetic analysis for the OSS of the emerging Soviet geopolitical threat to the Western democracies. After the war, he expanded his secret OSS paper into a book entitled *The Struggle for the World* that was published in 1947 during the same week that the President of the United States announced the aid program to Greece and Turkey that became known as the Truman Doctrine.

It was in *The Struggle for the World* and in a previous essay entitled "Lenin's Heir" in the liberal anti-communist journal *Partisan Review* that Burnham first manifested the influence on his thought of the great British global geopolitical theorist, Sir Halford Mackinder. Burnham warned his countrymen and the West that the Soviet Union sought to achieve effective political control of Eastern Europe, all of Eurasia, and Mackinder's "World-Island" (Eurasia-Africa) and, thereby, dominate the world. Containment, he explained in two subsequent books, *The Coming Defeat of Communism* (1949) and *Containment or Liberation?* (1951), was a defensive strategy that would not enable the West to win the Cold War. Instead, he wrote, the United States should adopt a policy of "liberation" that would seek to undermine Soviet power in Eastern Europe and elsewhere by exploiting the inherent vulnerabilities of the communist system.

"By the early 1950s," writes Kelly, "Burnham's prescriptions had become Cold War orthodoxy for conservatives, and in 1952 the GOP drew heavily on them for its foreign policy plank, which demanded an end to containment and a strategy of 'rolling back' communism." Burnham also became a consultant to the newly created Central Intelligence Agency (CIA) and joined the Cold War cultural front by his involvement with the Congress of Cultural Freedom (CCF). Both the CIA and CCF were dominated by liberal anti-communist intellectuals, a group that Burnham eventually broke with over the issue of domestic communism and what became known as "McCarthyism."

Burnham, according to Kelly, although not a defender of Senator McCarthy, was an "anti-anti-McCarthyite." Kelly quotes Burnham's letter of resignation from the editorial advisory board of *Partisan Review*: "I do not regard myself as either 'pro-McCarthy' or 'anti-McCarthy,'" he wrote. "I approve of many things that McCarthy has done, and certain of his methods; I disapprove some of his actions, and a number of his methods. But," Burnham continued, "'McCarthyism' is not McCarthy. I believe 'McCarthyism' to be an invention of the Communist tacticians, who launched it and are exploiting it, exactly as they have done on the case of a dozen of their previous operations in what might be called diversionary semantics."

Increasingly unwelcome among the anti-communist Left, Burnham began writing for conservative magazines such as the *Freeman* and the *American Mercury*. In 1954, he wrote a book about communist infiltration of the U.S. government in the 1930s and 1940s, entitled *The Web of Subversion*. One year later, he joined the editorial staff of William F. Buckley, Jr's new magazine, *National Review*, where he worked for the next twenty-three years.

Kelly devotes almost half of the book to Burnham's work at *National Review*, where he served as both a senior editor and a regular columnist. His column on the Cold War reported and analyzed the major events of the long struggle: the Hungarian uprising, the Suez Crisis, Quemoy and Matsu, Sputnik, the Bay of Pigs, the Berlin Wall, the Cuban Missile Crisis, the war in Southeast Asia, the Czech uprising, détente, arms control, the Arab-Israeli wars in 1967 and 1973, the Sino-Soviet split, Nixon's opening to China, Angola, and much more. His influence on the magazine's editorial positions and policies was second to none. William F. Buckley, Jr. credited Burnham with being the "dominant intellectual influence" of the magazine.

Burnham wrote his last major book, *Suicide of the West*, in 1964. Kelly calls it "the most uneven of Burnham's books," but also praises it as "the first attempt at a comprehensive study...of American liberalism in the middle of the twentieth century." In the book, Burnham warned that Western Civilization was in the process of committing suicide, and he called liberalism the "ideology of Western suicide." But he did not blame liberalism for being the cause of Western suicide. "The cause or causes," Burnham explained, "have something to do...with the decay of religion and with an excess of material luxury; and with getting tired, worn out as all things temporal do."

Suicide of the West was a brilliant dissection of the tenets of modern liberalism. Kelly notes that it "faithfully captured the liberalism of the 1970s and 1980s." Burnham also accurately sensed that the United States and the Western democracies were headed for a period of imperial retreat, which manifested itself in the 1970s in the wake of the U.S. defeat in Vietnam. By the time the United States recovered from that global retreat, in the early 1980s under the leadership of President Ronald Reagan, Burnham had stopped writing after suffering a stroke.

In the Foreword to Kelly's book, current *National Review* senior editor Richard Brookhiser credits President Reagan for the fall of the Soviet Empire, and indirectly credits Burnham for helping to lay the intellectual foundation that resulted in Reagan's rise to power. Kelly, however, will have none of this. The Soviet Union, he writes, collapsed not as a result of a "Western offensive policy," but because of "structural flaws that rotted the Soviet system...." Here, Brookhiser is closer to the truth than Kelly about both Reagan and Burnham. But

Brookhiser, too, misses a fundamental intellectual connection between Reagan and Burnham.

In the late 1940s and early 1950s, Burnham proposed an elaborate U.S. offensive strategy to exploit Soviet vulnerabilities so as to weaken and eventually undermine the Soviet Empire. In the 1980s, as we have learned from Peter Schweizer and others, Reagan changed U.S. policy vis-à-vis the Soviet Empire from the flaccid containment (called "détente") of the Nixon-Ford-Carter years to a more offensive political strategy designed to undermine Soviet power. While there is no direct evidence that Reagan or his national security advisers consciously adopted Burnham's proposed strategy of liberation, it is unquestionably true that Reagan's policies in the 1980s were generally consistent with the thrust of Burnham's strategy. We know that, based on Reagan's own writings and speeches, and his selection of Burnham in 1983 as a recipient of the Presidential Medal of Freedom, Reagan was familiar with Burnham's intellectual career and was a devoted reader of *National Review*. There is, then, at least a circumstantial link between Reagan's confrontational policies toward the Soviets in the 1980s and Burnham's proposed strategy of "liberation" that was first conceived in the late 1940s.

Kelly rightly concludes that Burnham's intellectual stature never fully recovered from his break with the Left over "McCarthyism." His name and his writings, sadly, are largely unknown to the American public. Few of today's neo-conservatives recognize the intellectual debt they owe to Burnham. Like them, he traveled the intellectual road from Left to Right, but unlike them he did so ar a time when liberalism was the dominant force in American intellectual life. As Kelly writes, Burnham deserves to be remembered as "a singular thinker," someone who "excelled as a political analyst," and as "one of his era's most remarkable political intelligences." "[H]e should be ranked," continues Kelly, "among the more acute interpreters of his time."

Inchon and the Course of U.S. Foreign Policy

Inchon! Among military historians and scholars, the name Inchon connotes daring, audacity and military genius. Fifty-eight years ago, on September 15, 1950, U.S. military forces, led by the 1st Marine Division, seized that strategic South Korean port, moved swiftly inland to take Kimpo Airfield, and by the end of September, after intense and bloody fighting, took Seoul, the South Korean capital, from communist forces. The amphibious landing at Inchon achieved tactical and strategic surprise. At one brilliant stroke, the Inchon landing relieved the pressure on the remaining U.S. and South Korean forces dug-in at the Pusan perimeter, severed the North Korean supply lines, and forced the communist forces into a headlong retreat across the 38th parallel. The U.S. victory at Inchon, however, also set the stage for a dramatic debate about the direction and goals of U.S. foreign policy in the early Cold War period; a debate that initially revolved around the forceful personalities of General of the Army Douglas MacArthur and President Harry S. Truman.

MacArthur was 70 years old at the time of the Inchon landing. His distinguished fifty-year military career included deputy command and command of the "Rainbow Division" in France during the First World War where he was repeatedly decorated for heroism and bravery; superintendent of the U.S. Military Academy at West Point; Army Chief of Staff in the early 1930s; military advisor to the Philippines and command of the nascent Filipino army; commander of U.S. and allied forces in the Southwest Pacific during World War II where he was awarded the Congressional Medal of Honor; and military governor of Japan in the immediate post-World War II years.

MacArthur conceived the Inchon landing after visiting the battlefront on a hill near the south bank of the Han River on June 29, 1950, four days after the North Korean invasion. In his memoirs, MacArthur recalled that he "watched for an hour the pitiful evidence of the disaster I had inherited. In that brief interval on the blood-soaked hill, I formulated my plans." "I would rely," he continued, "upon strategic maneuver to overcome the great odds against me."[1]

During the Second World War, MacArthur had planned and launched more than fifty successful amphibious envelopments of enemy forces in the Southwest Pacific. Despite that record of success, however, his Inchon plan met with stiff resistance and repeated doubts in Washington. Members of the Joint Chiefs of Staff, Marine and Naval officers repeatedly emphasized the great risks posed by the narrow port channel and the extremely high tides at Inchon. At the decisive conference on August 23rd at MacArthur's headquarters in Tokyo, MacArthur patiently listened for an hour to these and other expressions of doubt. He later recalled, "I could almost hear my father's voice telling me as he had so many years before, 'Doug, councils of war breed timidity and defeatism.'"[2] Then, for the next thirty minutes or so, MacArthur forcefully argued that the only alternative to the Inchon landing would be to slug it out in a costly war of attrition. "Are you content," he asked the doubters, "to let our troops stay in that bloody perimeter like beef cattle in the slaughterhouse?" He ended his presentation in dramatic fashion: "We shall land at Inchon and I shall crush them."[3]

The Inchon landing produced precisely the results promised by MacArthur. Soon, South Korea was cleared of communist forces, and U.S. and UN forces crossed the 38th parallel into North Korea. The Truman administration and the UN proclaimed a policy of liberating and unifying all of Korea under non-communist leadership. Truman flew to Wake Island in October to reap the political benefits of MacArthur's victory at Inchon.

In late October-early November, however, Chinese communist forces surged across the Yalu River and halted the U.S. and allied advance. It was a massive intelligence failure. MacArthur advised Washington, "We face an entirely new war," and proposed to defeat Chinese forces and achieve the liberation of all of Korea. Truman, however, ultimately retreated from the earlier goal of liberation, and Washington increasingly imposed restrictions on MacArthur's ability to wage war against Chinese forces. MacArthur publicly complained about those restrictions. U.S. and allied forces were pushed back across the 38th parallel. The war settled into a bloody stalemate. But MacArthur believed, as he wrote to a Republican congressman, that in war "there is no substitute for victory." MacArthur hinted at the possible use of atomic weapons. When in April 1951 MacArthur issued an ultimatum to China to surrender or face defeat at the same time that Truman was attempting to negotiate a cease-fire with China, Truman fired the General.

MacArthur came home to a hero's welcome. In a dramatic address to congress and in subsequent congressional hearings, MacArthur sharply criticized Truman's policy of limited war in Korea. The Joint Chiefs of Staff, however, backed Truman, calling a potential expanded war with China, the wrong war, at the wrong time, with the wrong enemy. Truman had settled for containing communist expansion instead of liberating areas under communist control.

The Truman-MacArthur dispute reflected a wider strategic debate about the best method to wage the Cold War. The forces supporting MacArthur sided with the approach advanced by James Burnham, a leading anti-communist intellectual, in three influential books written between 1947-1951, *The Struggle for the World, The Coming Defeat of Communism*, and *Containment or Liberation?*. Burnham argued that the "World Communist Enterprise" headquartered in Moscow effectively controlled the geopolitical "Heartland" of the Eurasian landmass, and could only be defeated by an aggressive policy of "Liberation," which would free key areas from communist control, particularly Eastern Europe. Containment, Burnham contended, was too defensive and left it to the communists to determine where and when the conflict would be fought. During the 1952 presidential campaign and early in 1953, candidate and President Dwight Eisenhower paid lip service to a policy of Liberation or "rollback."

Those who sided with Truman in the dispute looked for intellectual support to George F. Kennan, a top State Department planner who had explained the policy of containment in an article in *Foreign Affairs* in 1947. Kennan had written that "firm and vigilant" containment would promote the eventual mellowing and break-up of Soviet power.

At stake in Korea, therefore, was not only the future of the Korean peninsula, but also the overall strategic direction of U.S. foreign policy in the Cold War. That became clear when the Joint Chiefs of Staff and key Truman foreign policy advisors squared-off against MacArthur in lengthy congressional hearings held in the wake of MacArthur's removal from command in Korea. While Truman remained in office, containment won out over liberation.

Events soon proved that Eisenhower, too, favored containment over liberation. Eisenhower ended the Korean War without liberating North Korea. When East Germans in 1953 and Hungarians in 1956 rose up against their communist oppressors and requested U.S. assistance, the Eisenhower administration stood by and watched as the Soviets and their allies crushed the rebellions. In the next decade, in Southeast Asia, Presidents Kennedy, Johnson and Nixon, following the Korean precedent, fought a limited war, choosing containment over liberation. The U.S. also stood-by while the Czechoslovakian communists crushed the Prague Spring in 1968.

Prior to Inchon, the debate about containment versus liberation was theoretical. Inchon and its aftermath forced U.S. policymakers to choose a strategy. For better or worse, they chose containment.

ENDNOTES

1. Douglas MacArthur, *Reminiscences* (New York: McGraw-Hill Book Company, 1964), p. 333.

2. *Ibid.* at p. 349.

3. D. Clayton James, *The Years of MacArthur: Triumph & Disaster 1945-1964* (Boston: Houghton Mifflin Company, 1985), p. 470.

Arms Races, Arms Control, and the History of the Cold War

Patrick Glynn, a former arms control adviser to the Reagan administration and currently a resident scholar at the American Enterprise Institute, was among a handful of strategic thinkers in the 1980s who criticized U.S. and Western arms control efforts in a systematic and comprehensive manner. Writing in such journals as *Commentary* and *The National Interest*, Glynn marshaled facts and presented arguments which revealed flaws, not only in specific arms control treaties, agreements and proposals, but also in the underlying logic and theories of Western arms control proponents. In his book, *Closing Pandora's Box: Arms Races, Arms Control and the History of the Cold War*, Glynn broadens his approach by critically reviewing the major attempts at arms control in the twentieth century.

Glynn begins by demolishing what he calls the "Sarajevo fallacy"—the widespread belief, fostered by revisionist historians, that the First World War resulted largely from an arms competition among the European great powers. This belief, which persists to this day and which ignores the compelling evidence that the war was caused by Germany's attempt to upset the European balance of power, was destined to have lasting consequences in that, according to Glynn, it "laid the basic theoretical foundations of modern thinking about arms races and arms control." Glynn points out that World War I was preceded but not prevented by intense efforts at naval arms control by Britain and Germany. "[T]he arms negotiations failed," writes Glynn, "because the underlying cause of the arms race lay beyond the power of diplomats to remedy, since it went to the very nature of German ambitions and the German regime." In other words, the war resulted from *political* differences and disputes among the great powers which fueled the arms race, not from the arms race itself.

Memories of the terrible slaughter of the First World War produced a flurry of disarmament activities during the 1920s and 1930s. The Treaty of Versailles imposed restrictions on German armaments and established a commission to monitor German compliance. The Washington Naval Treaty of 1922 set limits on the numbers and ratios of battleships that could be built by the U.S., Britain, and Japan. In 1928, sixty-two nations signed the Kellogg-Briand Pact wherein they pledged to refrain from using war as an instrument of national policy. The London Naval Treaty of 1930 imposed further restrictions on naval powers. A disarmament conference was held in Geneva in 1932. Meanwhile, Germany, Soviet Russia, and Japan rearmed at a faster pace than the status quo powers. As Glynn points out, the mere fact that nations rearmed did not bring about the Second World War. It was, rather, the *political* objectives of Germany, the USSR, and Japan that produced the war, and those political objectives drove the arms race of the 1920s and 1930s.

The valuable "lessons of Munich"—that an aggressive, revolutionary dictatorship's expansionist aims should be resisted, not appeased—were, for many statesmen and observers, rendered irrelevant by the advent of nuclear weapons and the beginning of the Cold War. Glynn recounts and analyzes the numerous arms control treaties and disarmament proposals and schemes of the Cold War period: the Baruch Plan of 1946; the effort to convince President Truman to forego development of the H-bomb; Eisenhower's "Open Skies" proposals; the Limited Test Ban Treaty; the SALT I Treaty; the ABM Treaty; the SALT II talks; the START talks; the nuclear "freeze" and "no first use" proposals; the Reykjavik summit proposals; and the INF Treaty. The nuclear era, especially during and after the SALT talks, gave birth to an "arms control establishment" both within and outside the U.S. government which pursued arms control for its own sake, without reference to the larger geopolitical context. One of the great virtues of Glynn's book is that it deals with specific arms control agreements and proposals within a broad historical and geopolitical framework. Another virtue, also absent from the arms control establishment's world view, is Glynn's recognition that throughout the Cold War perceptions of the nuclear balance affected political events and crises.

Glynn's historical account of arms races and arms control reveals many instances of poor statesmanship on the part of such arms control enthusiasts as Ramsey MacDonald, Robert McNamara, Paul Warnke, Cyrus Vance, Henry Kissinger, and former Presidents Nixon and Carter. The heroes of Glynn's book, i.e., those political figures who resisted the arms control *zeitgeist*, include Winston Churchill, Senator Henry "Scoop" Jackson, and former President Ronald Reagan. In fact, Glynn argues that Reagan's SDI program and his refusal to sacrifice it for the sake of signing an arms control agreement played an important role in causing the collapse of the Soviet Empire.

Glynn mentions, but does not fully develop, a factor which would have further bolstered his argument against arms control. Soviet military writings dating from the early 1960s through the 1980s evidenced a doctrinal preference for a war-winning nuclear strategy totally at odds with the U.S. concept of "mutual assured destruction." But, like so many other factors and details that did not fit neatly into the arms control proponents' theories and world view, those Soviet military writings were largely ignored.

The end of the Cold War does not mean the end of arms control. Russia is still a nuclear weapons superpower. Furthermore, it seems likely that more countries will in the future acquire nuclear weapons and ballistic missile technology. That being so, Glynn's book offers these important insights gleaned from the history of arms control in this century: (1) disarmament agreements have not resolved political disputes between nations, and have never prevented wars; (2) arms control treaties have created unrealizable expectations among democratic populations, often resulting in dangerous illusions about potential adversaries; (3) arms control schemes have developed a momentum of their own which led proponents to ignore or downplay problems of verifiability and non-compliance; (4) arms control frequently has been used by adversaries to undermine the resolve and thereby weaken democratic powers; and (5) the pursuit of arms control divorced from the larger historical and geopolitical context has led to unpreparedness and war.

Henry M. Jackson: Hero of the Cold War

The 1970s was the most dangerous decade of the Cold War for the United States and the West. Domestic divisions resulting from the war in Southeast Asia shattered the post-World War II foreign policy consensus, while Watergate sapped the authority and will of U.S. Presidents to confront Soviet aggression. The decade that began with our slow, painful withdrawal from Vietnam, ended with the Soviet invasion of Afghanistan and the humiliation of the Iranian hostage crisis. By 1980, what the Soviets called "the correlation of forces" was shifting ominously in their favor.

The policy that throughout the 1970s reconciled the United States to Soviet gains in the Cold War was called "détente," and détente's chief critic in the U.S. government was the junior Senator from the state of Washington, Henry M. "Scoop" Jackson. Throughout that decade, from his influential perch on the Armed Services Committee, Jackson, as detailed in Robert Kaufman's excellent new biography *Henry M. Jackson: A Life in Politics*, tirelessly exposed the weak and conceptually flawed assumptions underlying the policy of détente. Jackson charged, and used committee and subcommittee hearings to show, that under détente the Soviets: used arms control negotiations to gain strategic advantages over the U.S.; repeatedly violated arms control agreements; acquired much needed grain and militarily useful technology from the West; and, relentlessly, but cautiously, pursued a geopolitical offensive.   "Jackson's critique of détente," writes Kaufman, "anticipated and inspired the conservative and neo-conservative challenge to détente that reached its apotheosis with the presidency of Ronald Reagan."

Indeed, Jackson's impact on Reagan's national security policy manifested itself by Reagan's appointments of Richard Perle, Jeane Kirkpatrick, Elliot Abrams, Max Kampelman, Paul Wolfowitz, Richard Pipes, Edward Rowny, John Lehman, Joshua Muravchik, and Frank Gaffney to key defense and foreign policy positions in his administration. Those "Jackson Democrats" (many of whom served at one time on Jackson's staff) helped formulate and implement the policies that, arguably, resulted in the collapse of the Soviet Empire.

Henry Jackson's Cold War journey began in November 1945 when as a congressman he traveled to Copenhagen as President Truman's representative to the International Labor Organization meeting. After the meeting, Jackson stopped in Norway, his parents' birthplace, where he encountered widespread expressions of fear of the Soviet Union. "The fears Norwegians expressed about their Soviet neighbors," Kaufman believes, "planted the seed in Jackson's mind that Soviet totalitarianism had replaced the defeated, discredited Nazi version as the primary threat to civilization." Jackson subsequently supported in Congress Truman's programs to aid Greece and Turkey (the Truman Doctrine) and Western Europe (the Marshall Plan). He enthusiastically supported the Berlin Airlift and the formation of NATO. In January 1949, House Speaker Sam Rayburn selected Jackson to sit on the Joint Committee on Atomic Energy, an appointment that Kaufman calls "the launching pad for establishing his reputation as an expert on defense and foreign policy issues." The same year, Jackson, in the face of strong opposition, urged Truman to build the hydrogen bomb. "Falling behind in the atomic armaments' competition," reasoned Jackson, "will mean national suicide." Jackson's role in the decision to build the hydrogen bomb, concludes Kaufman, "conditioned his responses to the great national debates over arms control, national security, and détente during the 1970s...."

During the 1950s and 1960s, Jackson remained steadfast in his support of measures designed to maintain the United States' ability to contain the Soviet Union, and equally steadfast in his opposition to proposals he believed would weaken our position vis-à-vis the Soviets. He supported the national security approach outlined in NSC-68; defended Truman's decision to resist communist aggression in Korea; advocated the development and deployment of nuclear submarines; and promoted the speedy development of intercontinental ballistic missiles and strategic bombers. At the same time, Jackson criticized the Eisenhower administration's over-reliance on nuclear weapons to deter Soviet aggression. He urged President Eisenhower to spend more on conventional forces, anticipating President Kennedy's policy of "flexible response." Amidst the euphoria of the "spirit of Geneva," Jackson warned Americans that the Kremlin viewed U.S.-Soviet summitry as "just another device in the Cold War arsenal."

Presidents Kennedy and Johnson received Jackson's general support for the build-up of nuclear and conventional forces and the war in Southeast Asia. But Jackson led the effort to attach reservations to Kennedy's Test Ban Treaty with the Soviets, clashed repeatedly with Defense Secretary McNamara over strategic nuclear policy and the conduct of the Vietnam War, and opposed efforts to scuttle the development and deployment of anti-ballistic missile systems. Jackson resisted the Democratic Party's move to the left on defense and foreign policy issues in the late 1960s, and that resistance grew stronger as the McGovernites gained control of the Party in the late 1960s and early 1970s. That courageous resistance doomed Jackson's two bids for the Party's nomination for the Presidency in the 1970s.

Although Jackson was unsuccessful in his Presidential bids in 1972 and 1976, the decade of the 1970s was his "finest hour." "During those tumultuous years," Kaufman explains, "he led the fight and offered the most compelling arguments against the policy of détente as Presidents Richard Nixon, Gerald Ford, and Jimmy Carter practiced it; at the same time, he waged an increasingly lonely battle against the isolationist impulse then regnant in the national Democratic Party." That the Soviet Union did not win the Cold War in the 1970s is attributable, in part, to Henry Jackson. Former Senator and Reagan Chief of Staff Howard Baker said it best: "Jackson made sure we did not lose the Cold

War during the 1970s so that Ronald Reagan could win it in the 1980s." In every sense, Henry Jackson was a hero of the Cold War.

Solzhenitsyn: The Most Consequential Writer of the 20th Century

Toward the end of the Second World War, a captain in the Soviet Army exchanged letters with a colleague that included unkind references to Soviet dictator Josef Stalin ("big shot" and "the moustachioed one"). On February 9, 1945, in the village of Wormdit, near Konigsberg, this "offense" against the Soviet state resulted in the soldier's arrest and imprisonment for eight years in a slave-labor camp and, ironically, began the literary career of the most consequential writer of the 20th century—a writer who "spoke the truth to power" and thereby helped inspire and marshal the forces that eventually led to the demise of the Soviet state.

That writer, Aleksandr Solzhenitsyn, died on August 3, 2008, at the age of 89. Solzhenitsyn wrote numerous works of fiction and non-fiction, including *One Day in the Life of Ivan Denisovich, The First Circle, Cancer Ward, August 1914, Lenin in Zurich, The Oak and the Calf, Warning to the West, From Under the Rubble, November 1916, Invisible Allies,* and *The Mortal Danger.* But the work that made him the most consequential writer of the 20th century was the massive, three-volume *Gulag Archipelago.*

Solzhenitsyn's life and literary career benefited from Stalin's death in 1953 and the so-called Khrushchev "thaw" that followed. Many political prisoners like Solzhenitsyn were released from the labor camps, some of the crimes of Stalin were publicized and condemned, and censorship was somewhat eased. This environment enabled Solzhenitsyn in 1962 to publish his first fictional critique of the Soviet labor camp system, *One Day in the Life of Ivan Denisovich.*

After Khrushchev's fall from power in 1964, Solzhenitsyn tried to publish two more fictional books, *The First Circle* and *Cancer Ward,* which were highly critical of the Stalin era. Khrushchev's successor as General Secretary of the Communist Party, Leonid Breszhnev, and his Politburo colleagues, however, rightly worried that Solzhenitsyn's criticisms of the Party could extend beyond Stalin to the very heart of the Soviet system. Literary censorship was tightened. The manuscripts were refused publication by state authorities. They began circulating in *samizdat,* secretly, underground, in typewritten form. Solzhenitsyn also smuggled out copies to the West. He was increasingly viewed by the Communist Party as an enemy of the state who had to be silenced or removed.

Initially unbeknownst to the Soviet security services, Solzhenitsyn was also secretly at work on a lengthy examination of the origins and history of the forced labor camp system known by its Russian acronym, GULAG. Working with allies both within and outside the Soviet Union, Solzhenitsyn, under constant harassment and surveillance by the security services, successfully smuggled out of the Soviet Union his manuscript of *The Gulag Archipelago* which was initially published in France and then elsewhere in the West in the early and mid 1970s.

The English translation of *The Gulag Archipelago* appeared during 1973-1978 and runs to 1,821 pages in three volumes. The first volume explored the experiences of arrest, interrogation, detention, and transit to the camps. Volume two traced the history of the camp system beginning in Lenin's time with the early prisons on Solovetsky Island in the White Sea, and later throughout the Soviet Union as the Gulag "metastasized" under Stalin. This volume, perhaps the most memorable of the three, goes inside the camps to explore all aspects of camp life: the harsh conditions of labor; the extreme climates; the unsanitary conditions; the lack of adequate food; the brutality of camp guards; friendships, loyalties, love, treachery, thievery, and kindnesses among the camp inmates or *zeks*; life, suffering, and death.

The final volume explored the unquenchable spirit of resistance among many camp inmates (escapes, rebellions, acts of martyrdom), the downscaling of the camp system after Stalin's death, the experience of leaving the camps and being transferred to forced internal exile, and, finally, attaining "liberty." Volume three, however, closed with the sobering reality that in the Soviet system, "rulers change, the Archipelago remains." "The same treacherous secrecy, the same fog of injustice," Solzhenitsyn wrote, "still hangs in our air...For a half century and more the enormous state has towered over us, girded us with hoops of steel. The hoops are still there. There is no law."

The Gulag Archipelago, therefore, was more than a denunciation of Stalin. It laid bare the rot at the core of the Soviet system. And it traced that rot all the way back to Lenin, who at the time was still revered by many intellectuals in the West. Even worse, it claimed, notwithstanding rhetorical pronouncements of détente and "peaceful coexistence," that fundamentally the system had not changed with Stalin's death, as some in the West believed.

Solzhenitsyn's masterpiece surfaced in the West just as Western leaders were embarked on the decade-long, futile, and often self-defeating policy toward the Soviet Union known as détente. Détente so corroded the moral fiber of some Western leaders that it led the State Department to advise President Gerald Ford to refuse to invite Solzhenitsyn to the White House (after he was forcibly exiled from Russia) for fear of offending Soviet leaders. "Not even Watergate," wrote columnist George Will, "was as *fundamentally* degrading to the presidency as this act of deference to the master of the Gulag Archipelago."

Unwelcome at the White House, Solzhenitsyn was invited by AFL-CIO President George Meany to address the labor organization in Washington on June 30, 1975, an address later included in a book called *Warning to the West*. In the speech, he ridiculed détente, contending that "The Soviet Union has used détente, is using it now, and will continue to use it in its own interests." "Nothing has changed in Communist ideology," he warned. "The goals are the same as they were, but instead of the artless Khrushchev, who couldn't hold his tongue ('we will bury you'), now they say 'Détente.'" "Communist leaders," he continued, "respect only firmness and have contempt for persons who continually give in to them." Détente, he said, was "a process of shortsighted concessions; a process of giving up and giving up and giving up in the hope that perhaps at some point the wolf will have eaten enough."

In that same speech, however, Solzhenitsyn pointed to a phenomenon which would in the long run undermine Soviet rule. "Under the cast-iron shell of Communism," he explained, "a liberation of the human spirit is occurring. New generations are growing up, steadfast in their struggle with evil, unwilling to accept unprincipled compromises, preferring to lose everything...so as not to sacrifice conscience, unwilling to make deals with evil."

With this and similar speeches in the U.S. and Britain, Solzhenitsyn confronted the statesmen of the West with the consequences of their own moral blindness and strategic shortsightedness. Three years later, in his commencement address at Harvard, Solzhenitsyn confronted the U.S. liberal intelligentsia and elites and many other Americans with the consequences of their moral cowardice and spiritual bankruptcy. Abroad, Solzhenitsyn lamented, this lack of courage and willpower led to the tragedy of our defeat in Vietnam and the consequent horrors for the Vietnamese and Cambodian people, and a moral feebleness in dealing with powerful countries such as China and the Soviet Union and international terrorists. At home, the decline of religion and the promotion of limitless personal freedom led to moral squalor and a neglect and often rejection of the civilizing heritage of Christianity.

In 1980, with détente in shatters after the Soviet invasion of Afghanistan, Cuban troops in Africa, and communists in control in Nicaragua, Solzhenitsyn wrote *The Mortal Danger: How Misconceptions About Russia Imperil America*, which originally appeared as an article in the journal *Foreign Affairs*. This was a scathing attack on "Sovietology" as practiced by Western diplomats, statesmen, and scholars, including George Kennan, Henry Kissinger, and, surprisingly, Richard Pipes. The West was in mortal danger, he wrote, because of "sixty years of obstinate blindness to the true nature of communism."

"Communism," he wrote, "will never be halted by negotiations or through the machinations of détente. It can be halted only by force from without or by disintegration from within." Solzhenitsyn's principal message in the book, however, was that the West's best allies in the Cold War struggle against Soviet communism were the peoples—including Russians—held captive by Soviet rule.

In a speech in the U.S. Senate chamber in 1975, which was published in *Warning to the West*, Solzhenitsyn told his audience that, "Very soon...your country will stand in need of not just exceptional men but of *great* men. Find them in your souls. Find them in your hearts. Find them in the depths of your country." Nineteen years later, Solzhenitsyn, writing in *National Review*, recalled those words and added, "Five years later, I was overjoyed when just such a man came to the White House."

Ronald Reagan campaigned for the presidency in 1976 as the nation's chief critic of détente. Four years later, his election to the White House was in part due to the obvious failure of détente. As president, he initiated policies that attacked the vulnerabilities of the Soviet system and helped undermine its rule in

Eastern Europe and Russia. Reagan proved Solzhenitsyn right: the communist system could only be halted by force from without or by disintegration from within.

And just as Reagan proved Solzhenitsyn right, Solzhenitsyn proved the truth of Norman Podhortetz's profound insight, written before the end of the Cold War, into the nature and value of Solzhenitsyn's moral challenge to the West:

> For here...is a lone individual who, by having successfully stood up to the full power of the Soviet state, has made himself into a living reproach to the West: a parable in action of the very courage in the face of Communist totalitarianism that the West has been unable or unwilling to summon in its own dealings with the Soviet state. Solzhenitsyn's terrible and terrifying question to us is this: is it possible that courage like his own is all we require to escape from the fate he has come to warn us against? Is it possible that the courage first to see the truth about Communism and then the correlative courage to act upon it can guide our steps to safety as his own courage guided Solzhenitsyn's, that it can make the Soviet leaders back down and ultimately, perhaps, even collapse, just as they did when confronted by Solzhenitsyn himself?
>
> Forcing us to face that terrible question, rubbing our noses in it, has been Solzhenitsyn's prophetic mission to the West.

The prophet is dead, but we honor his memory because he helped change the world for the better.

Ronald Reagan and the Collapse of the Soviet Empire

Ronald Reagan's death has revived debates about why the Cold War ended when it did, and what, if any, credit should go to Reagan for the collapse of the Soviet Empire. U.S. policy toward the Soviet Union during the Cold War is often portrayed as a steady, consistent application of the containment doctrine, which was first explained in George F. Kennan's 1947 article in *Foreign Affairs*, "The Sources of Soviet Conduct." In reality, however, U.S. Cold War policies differed in important respects from president to president.

The Truman administration initially combined overt resistance to Soviet encroachments in Europe with covert efforts to undermine Soviet power in Eastern and Central Europe. Diplomatic pressure in Iran, the Marshall Plan, the Truman Doctrine, the Berlin Airlift, financial assistance to non-communist parties in Western Europe, and the formation of NATO--all of which were designed to contain the spread of Soviet communism--were complemented with psychological, political and guerilla tactics behind the iron curtain. Truman's key policy document, NSC-68, envisioned an offensive strategy to defeat the Soviet Empire. American strategy, according to NSC-68, sought to "induce a retraction of the Kremlin's control and influence," and to "foster the seeds of destruction within the Soviet system." When Soviet-backed North Korean forces invaded South Korea in June 1950, the U.S.-led United Nations forces not only resisted the attack, but sought, with Truman's initial blessing, to liberate all of Korea from communist control. When communist Chinese forces intervened on a massive scale in October-November 1950, Truman, much to the chagrin of U.N and American commander, General Douglas MacArthur, abandoned the policy of liberating Korea and settled for containment.

The early Eisenhower administration gave lip service to a policy of "rolling back" the Soviet Empire. Eisenhower's Secretary of State, John Foster Dulles, had promoted such a policy prior to assuming office. In a 1950 memo to Senator Robert Taft, Dulles advocated "stimulating guerilla and insurrectional activities" within Eastern Europe, and "stepping up subversive activities within areas of Soviet control." Dulles subsequently wrote an article that appeared in *Life* magazine in which he publicly argued for a more offensive strategy vis-à-vis the Soviets. After Eisenhower took office, administration spokesmen publicly encouraged the enslaved nations of Eastern and Central Europe to rise up against their Soviet masters. When that actually happened in East Germany in 1953, and in Poland and Hungary in 1956, however, the United States did nothing to aid the resistance forces. In Korea, moreover, Eisenhower, like Truman, settled for containment. "Rollback" was shown to be merely empty rhetoric. Eisenhower, instead, relied on defensive security pacts with nations on the periphery of the Soviet Empire, and the threat of massive nuclear retaliation to hold the Soviets at bay on the Eurasian periphery. John F. Kennedy's presidency combined inspiring rhetoric about promoting liberty throughout the world ("bear any burden," "pay any price") with a reckless amateurism in the conduct of foreign policy. That amateurism led to the Bay of Pigs fiasco, the failed summit with Khrushchev in Vienna, the unsuccessful attempts to assassinate Cuban dictator Fidel Castro, the empty response to the construction of the Berlin Wall, the undermining of Diem in South Vietnam, and the promotion of arms control as a key element in U.S.-Soviet relations. Kennedy and his advisers ("the best and the brightest") moved energetically from crisis to crisis, and time and again, in the words of a recent historian of the Cold War, "energy...outstripped wisdom." Even the one arguably significant Cold War accomplishment of the Kennedy administration, the removal of Soviet missiles from Cuba, was a "negative" victory in that it merely pushed back a Soviet advance. And Kennedy paid a significant price for that negative victory by publicly promising to refrain from invading Cuba, which served as a Soviet base in the Western Hemisphere for the next twenty-seven years, and by secretly agreeing to remove U.S. missiles from Turkey.

The Johnson administration fought the Vietnam War encumbered by what James Burnham called the "self-imposed strategic prison" of containment. U.S. strategy throughout the conflict was *defensive*—to prevent a communist takeover of South Vietnam, not to liberate the North from communist rule. Containment also dictated Johnson's unwillingness to aid the popular uprising in Czechoslovakia in 1968, which consequently was crushed by Soviet troops. The Soviets had learned the lesson of 1956: containment meant that the U.S. would shrink from attempting to exploit vulnerabilities within the Soviet Empire. It was a straight line from containment to the so-called "Brezhnev doctrine" which proclaimed that once a state or territory fell under Soviet control, it would remain under Soviet control.

U.S. Cold War policy during the Nixon-Ford years de-emphasized the ideological component of the U.S.-Soviet conflict and sought to foster cooperation. This policy—called "détente"—emphasized arms control, trade agreements, superpower summitry, and an overall "lessening of tension" between the superpowers. Containment, to be sure, was still part of U.S. policy, as evidenced by the nuclear alert ordered by Nixon in response to threats of Soviet intervention during the Arab-Israeli War in 1973, and the courting of China as a *de facto* strategic ally against the Soviet Union. But détente helped to ideologically disarm the West by fostering illusions about the nature of Soviet communism. Détente's consequences included U.S. acquiescence to the loss of strategic nuclear superiority, a willingness to overlook Soviet cheating on arms control agreements, the U.S. abandonment of longtime allies in Southeast Asia, and formal recognition—in the Helsinki Accords—of a Soviet sphere of influence in Central and Eastern Europe. Nothing better symbolized the loss of American confidence and will during the years of détente than President Ford's unwillingness to welcome Soviet dissident Aleksandr Solzhenitsyn to the White House for fear of offending Soviet leaders.

President Jimmy Carter pursued détente to its logical extreme. In Carter's first major foreign policy address, he proclaimed that the U.S. had abandoned its "inordinate fear of communism." Longtime allies in the Cold War, such as the

Shah in Iran and Somoza in Nicaragua, were tossed aside or abandoned because of human rights violations, only to be replaced by more brutal regimes that pursued anti-American foreign policies. Carter signed arms control agreements with the Soviets that were so flawed that even a Senate controlled by his own political party refused to ratify them. Carter revealed the extent of his ignorance about the nature of the Soviet system when he expressed his disappointment and surprise at Soviet behavior after the Red Army invaded Afghanistan. Under Carter, containment, while still surviving as an overall policy, reached its nadir.

Ronald Reagan shattered the illusions of détente by redefining the nature of the Cold War between the West and Soviet communism, and adopting a strategy that successfully exploited the vulnerabilities of the Soviet system. In the late 1970s, Reagan told Richard Allen, who would become his first National Security Adviser, that his long-term strategy for dealing with the Soviet Union was simple: we win, they lose. During the 1980 campaign, Reagan opined to Lou Cannon of the *Washington Post* that the Soviets lacked the economic wherewithal to compete in an all-out arms race with the West. After assuming office, Reagan proclaimed in April 1981 that the West "won't contain communism, it will transcend communism." The Soviet system, he said, was a "bizarre chapter in human history whose last pages are even now being written." The next year, Reagan told the British Parliament that he had a long term plan "which will leave Marxism-Leninism on the ash heap of history." In January 1983, Reagan signed National Security Decision Directive 75, which stated that U.S. policy was "[t]o contain and over time reverse Soviet expansionism..., [t]o promote...the process of change in the Soviet Union toward a more pluralistic political and economic system..., [to] exploit...vulnerabilities within the Soviet empire" in an effort to "loosen Moscow's hold" on Eastern Europe.

Reagan's offensive strategy included providing aid to anti-communist rebels in Afghanistan, Nicaragua and elsewhere; supporting dissident groups and movements in Eastern Europe; toppling the Soviet-backed government in Grenada; tightening controls on the transfer of militarily useful technology to Eastern bloc countries; promoting SDI; a massive U.S. military build-up; and efforts to exploit Soviet economic difficulties.

In June 1987, Reagan challenged Soviet leader Mikhail Gorbachev to "tear down" the Berlin Wall. Two years later, the Wall came down, then the enslaved nations of the Soviet Empire gradually broke free, and the Soviet Union collapsed.

Reagan's predecessors, to be sure, deserve credit for keeping the Soviets at bay for more than thirty years. Soviet leader Mikhail Gorbachev also deserves credit for his unwillingness to forcibly crush the rebellion in the satellite nations during 1989-1991. Others who meaningfully contributed to the downfall of the Soviet Empire include Pope John Paul II, the courageous dissident groups within the Empire, and the Western armed forces who stood watch and sometimes fought on the Eurasian periphery and elsewhere during the "long twilight struggle." But when all is said and done, it was Ronald Reagan who seized the moment and instituted the right policies at the right time to bring about the Soviet collapse.

Ronald Reagan and the End of the Cold War

The once widely held conventional view that Ronald Reagan stumbled his way through the end of the Cold War by sheer good luck has been shattered by two recent books—one by a conservative scholar, and the other by a liberal intellectual historian. Together, these two books, building on the work of previous scholars since the collapse of the Soviet empire, catapult Reagan to the forefront of presidential greatness.

Paul Kengor's *The Crusader: Ronald Reagan and the Fall of Communism*, contends that Reagan's goal of defeating communism and winning the Cold War can be traced to his early struggles against communists in Hollywood as head of the Screen Actors Guild in the late 1940s. In this fight against an attempted communist takeover of the union, Reagan was, in the words of fellow actor Sterling Hayden, a "one man battalion."

Reagan continued to speak out against communism and the Soviet Union after he became a spokesperson for General Electric and a television personality, and when he entered the national political arena during the Goldwater presidential campaign in 1964. Kengor shows that from that time forward, Reagan consistently advocated winning the Cold War rather than settling for the "containment" of communism. For example, in 1950 Reagan joined the "Crusade for Freedom," a group that called for the roll back of the Soviet empire in Eastern Europe. He later gave speeches at anti-communist meetings and produced anti-communist television documentaries. In May of 1967, during a debate with Robert Kennedy, Reagan, anticipating what he would dramatically do as president twenty years later, called on Soviet leaders to bring down the Berlin Wall.

The Nixon-Ford-Kissinger approach to détente with the Soviet Union in the late 1960s and early 1970s, coupled with our defeat in the Vietnam War, weakened containment and caused Reagan to challenge Ford for the Republican nomination for president in 1976. Although Reagan narrowly lost the nomination, he and his followers controlled the GOP's foreign policy platform which all but abandoned the notion of détente.

President Jimmy Carter pursued détente with the Soviet Union even more vigorously than his predecessors. Carter set the tone of his approach to the Cold War by telling Americans that we were now free of our "inordinate fear of communism." Carter maintained that approach until the Soviet army invaded Afghanistan in December 1979 and shattered the president's remaining illusions about the nature of our communist adversary.

It is undisputed that when he became president, Ronald Reagan opposed détente and wanted to strengthen America's armed forces. But did he also have as a goal victory in the Cold War? And did he implement a concrete strategy for winning the Cold War? Or, as his detractors say, did Reagan just happen to be president when the Soviet empire collapsed due to internal problems unrelated to any of Reagan's policies?

The first scholar to significantly make the case that Ronald Reagan deliberately set out to win the Cold War was the Hoover Institution's Peter Schweizer. In two books—*Victory: The Reagan Administration's Secret Strategy That Hastened the Collapse of the Soviet Union* (1994) and *Reagan's War: The Epic Story of His Forty-Year Struggle and Final Triumph Over Communism* (2002)—Schweizer used interviews with some of Reagan's national security and foreign policy staffers, classified and declassified national security directives, Reagan's speeches and private correspondence, and documents from several foreign countries, to prove that Reagan intentionally abandoned détente, moved beyond a passive containment policy, and pursued a strategy of victory.

Schweizer noted that at the heart of Reagan's strategy was a sophisticated effort to exploit Soviet vulnerabilities, especially its economic vulnerabilities, which included: (1) covert financial and intelligence support to the Solidarity union in Poland and other opposition groups within the Soviet empire; (2) financial and military support to the Afghan resistance; (3) cooperative efforts with Saudi Arabia to drive down the price of oil, and limiting Soviet natural gas exports to the West, thereby reducing Soviet hard currency earnings; (4) a campaign to limit Soviet access to Western high technology; (5) a technological disinformation effort to help disrupt the Soviet economy; (6) a massive U.S. defense buildup, including the SDI program, to put more pressure on Soviet economic resources; and (7) financial, military and logistical support for anti-communist forces in several Third World countries. "Reagan," concluded Schweizer, "did have a well-developed plan seeking the demise of the Soviet Union."

Paul Kengor, a professor at Grove City College and the author of two books on the impact of religious belief on the presidencies of Reagan and George W. Bush, wholeheartedly agrees with Schweizer and, in *The Crusader*, builds on Schweizer's solid foundation to bolster the case for Reagan as the architect of the West's victory in the Cold War. According to Kengor, Reagan told staffers during the 1980 presidential campaign that his strategy for dealing with the Soviet Union was simple: "We win and they lose." In press interviews that same year, Reagan opined that the Soviets could not keep up with us in an all-out arms race, and that it was time for the United States to play that card in the Cold War struggle.

Kengor reveals that at the initial meeting of the new president's National Security Planning Group in January 1981, Reagan agreed with CIA Director William Casey's proposal that the U.S. confront the Soviet Union by exploiting the economic and political vulnerabilities of the communist empire. A secret Pentagon defense guidance issued shortly thereafter called for "reversing" Soviet expansion and encouraging long-term changes within the USSR.

On May 17, 1981, Reagan gave the first public hint of the new strategy in a speech at Notre Dame University. The West, he said, won't contain communism, it will transcend communism. "It will dismiss it," he explained, "as some bizarre chapter in human history *whose last pages are even now being written.*" A year later, in his Westminster address in England, Reagan spoke of a long-term "policy" that would leave communism "on the ash heap of history." Reagan noted that the Soviet Union was "in crisis," and "in deep economic difficulty," explaining that its political structure "no longer corresponds to its economic base."

Beginning in 1982, notes Kengor, Reagan and his national security team compiled Soviet vulnerability assessments and planned long-term economic warfare against the USSR. This included the super-secret "Farewell Dossier," which searched for the Soviet "Achilles heel," and devised a scheme to provide Soviet agents with defective technologies to sabotage Moscow's efforts to pilfer U.S. high technology research and products.

Reagan in 1982 and 1983 also approved a series of National Security Decision Directives (NSDDs) that launched economic warfare campaigns against Moscow, instituted political warfare programs designed to loosen the Kremlin's control of its satellite empire, and made it U.S. policy to bring about the collapse of the Soviet empire.

Viewed against this background, the massive U.S. military build-up, the promotion of SDI, the forcible liberation of Grenada from communist rule, assistance to anti-communist resistance forces within the Soviet empire and in the Third World, restrictions on high-technology transfers, and military assistance to the Afghan rebels, were all part of Reagan's successful crusade against Soviet communism.

Ronald Reagan, concludes Kengor, "was not content to contain Soviet Communism. He wanted to kill it. He not only said so but committed himself and his administration to that very deliberate goal—a goal that stemmed from Reagan himself, not his advisers, long before 1981."

If Kengor's Reagan is the great "crusader" against communism, John Patrick Diggins' Reagan is one of history's great "liberators," and is among the three or four greatest presidents in our nation's history. Diggins' new book, *Ronald Reagan: Fate, Freedom, and the Making of History*, is full of important insights into Reagan's character, and surprising judgments about Reagan's approach to the Cold War. Diggins admires Reagan and his role in ending the Cold War as much as Kengor does, but differs significantly from Kengor as to how Reagan ended the Cold War.

Diggins, the respected author of numerous works of intellectual history, calls Reagan our most "Emersonian" president, emphasizing Reagan's optimism, self-reliance, individualism, and political romanticism. Like Kengor, Diggins locates the roots of Reagan's anti-communism in the late 1940s struggle for control of the Screen Actors Guild and Hollywood. Reagan, Diggins explains, was also deeply influenced by the writings of F.A. Hayek and Whittaker Chambers. His anti-communism was further reinforced by the 1960s radical counter-culture which he opposed as California's governor.

Diggins contends that Reagan as president contributed to ending the Cold War, not by crusading against communism and exploiting Soviet vulnerabilities as urged by his neoconservative advisors, but by exercising prudent diplomacy and skillful statesmanship. "It is erroneous to argue," writes Diggins, "...that Reagan concluded that the time had come 'not merely to contain Communism but to defeat it.'" Instead, Reagan, motivated by a profound abhorrence at the prospect of nuclear war, ignored the advice of his more hawkish staffers and shifted from his early policy of emphasizing deterrence to a policy of dialogue. "Reagan broke free of the rigidities of cold war thinking," explains Diggins, "to begin negotiating with [Soviet leader] Gorbachev..." Thus, for Diggins, it was not Reagan's confrontational policies that caused the collapse of the Soviet empire, as Schweizer and Kengor claim, but rather his "enlightened statesmanship."

Reagan, according to Diggins, was not a conservative, but "the great liberating spirit of modern American history, a political romantic impatient with the status quo." He was not the "amiable dunce" of his detractors' imagination, but had "an intelligent, sensitive mind with passionate convictions." Reagan, Diggins explains, defied history and took control of events, and as a result, "[t]he cold war ended in an act of faith and trust, not fear and trembling."

Was Reagan the crusader of Kengor's book or the conciliator of Diggins' book? The answer, I believe, is that he was both. Reagan the crusader launched a political, military, psychological, and economic offensive designed to undermine Soviet power. Reagan's speeches, his national security directives, and his policies clearly were directed toward rolling-back the Soviet empire. Reagan the conciliator engaged in summitry and arms control negotiations with a new Soviet leadership in order to peacefully manage the endgame of the Cold War. The peoples of eastern and central Europe were, as a result, peacefully liberated from Soviet control.

The West's peaceful Cold War victory demonstrated that Reagan succeeded at being both a crusader and a conciliator, and the lifting of the "iron curtain" in eastern and central Europe fully justifies Diggins' claim that Reagan is one of the three great liberating presidents (Lincoln and FDR are the others) in our history.

The last word on this, however, goes not to Kengor or Diggins, but to perhaps the most thoughtful historian of the Cold War, John Lewis Gaddis. In his recently revised and updated *Strategies of Containment: A Critical Appraisal of American National Security Policy During the Cold War* (2005), Gaddis carefully concludes:

> What one can say now is that Reagan saw Soviet weaknesses sooner than most of his contemporaries did; that he understood the extent to which détente was perpetuating the Cold War rather than hastening its end; that his hard line strained the Soviet system at the moment of its maximum weakness; that his shift toward conciliation preceded Gorbachev; that he combined reassurance,

persuasion, and pressure in dealing with the new Soviet leader; and that he maintained the support of the American people and of American allies....Reagan's role here was critical.

Reagan, Gaddis explained, ended the Cold War by "changing rather than containing" the Soviet Union. "In doing so," writes Gaddis, "he resolved a contradiction that had bedeviled strategists of containment from the earliest days of the Cold War." That singular accomplishment surely warrants Reagan's placement among the greatest of U.S. presidents.

CHAPTER IV
The Post-Cold War World

The Grand Chessboard

Six years after the collapse of the Soviet empire, which ended the third global conflict of the 20th century, the United States, which emerged from the Cold War as the world's preeminent power, is still in search of a doctrine or world view to guide its statesmen in the post-Cold War era. In his book, *The Grand Chessboard*, Zbigniew Brzezinski, the former National Security Adviser to President Carter, attempts to fill that void by presenting a global geopolitical framework for the conduct of American foreign policy.

The importance of having a framework or "organizing principle" underlying the nation's foreign policy cannot be overstated. Such a framework or principle helps statesmen identify and distinguish between a nation's vital and enduring interests and its peripheral and transient ones. England's organizing principle in the 16th and 17th centuries, for example, was to prevent what is now Belgium from falling under the sway of a hostile power. As her empire expanded, so too did England's interests, which resulted in a new organizing principle: command of the sea and a more or less evenly balanced European continent. Finally, as her empire declined and her security became dependent on the United States, England's organizing principle became the "special relationship" with the U.S. and a strong NATO.

U.S. foreign policy has undergone a similar evolution. Initially, after winning the War of Independence, America's organizing principle was twofold: to eliminate European influence on the American continent and to expand westward ("Manifest Destiny"). As the nation expanded geographically its interests grew, and the Monroe Doctrine became the organizing principle of U.S. foreign policy. Henceforth, American statesmen sought to prevent the European great powers from interfering in the Western Hemisphere. U.S. overseas expansion into the Pacific and East Asia became the new organizing principle in the late 19th century, resulting in the Open Door policy, naval expansion and the construction of the Panama Canal. President Theodore Roosevelt's key role in ending the Russo-Japanese War and his sending of the fleet around the world signaled America's emergence as a great power. Finally, beginning with U.S. intervention in Europe in the First World War and continuing throughout the rest of the century, the organizing principle of American foreign policy has been to prevent the domination of Eurasia by a hostile power or coalition of powers.

Viewed in this light, the policy of "containment" was not the organizing principle of U.S. foreign policy from 1946-1991. Rather, containment was a *means* to implement the ongoing effort to prevent a hostile power from dominating Eurasia. Brzezinski's essential message in *The Grand Chessboard* is that even with the end of the Cold War, the organizing principle of U.S. foreign policy has not changed. The United States, he writes, "must consolidate and perpetuate the prevailing geopolitical pluralism on the map of Eurasia." U.S. policy must "make certain that no state or combination of states gains the capacity to expel the United States from Eurasia...."

For Brzezinski, Eurasia is "the grand chessboard," the central stage "on which the struggle for global primacy continues to be played...." That is because Eurasia, as Brzezinski points out, is by far the globe's largest continent, contains most of the world's population, accounts for 60% of the world's GNP and contains three-quarters of the world's known energy reserves. Brzezinski calls Eurasia the "supercontinent" and megacontinent," and subdivides it into four principal regions: a vast "middle space" which includes the territory of Russia and the newly independent states; a western region that includes Western and Central Europe; a southern region that encompasses the Middle East, the Persian Gulf area and Southwest Asia; and an eastern region that includes China, the Korean peninsula, Southeast Asia and Japan.

Brzezinski further identifies on Eurasia five "geostrategic players" and five "geopolitical pivots." He defines "geostrategic players" as "states that have the capacity and the national will to exercise power or influence beyond their borders in order to alter...the existing geopolitical state of affairs," and places in that category France, Germany, Russia, China and India (not Japan or Britain, surprisingly). "Geopolitical pivots," according to Brzezinski, are states "whose importance is derived...from their sensitive location and from the consequences of their potentially vulnerable condition" in relation to stronger powers. Ukraine, Azerbaijan, South Korea, Turkey and Iran are placed in that category.

There are also regions of Eurasia that, according to Brzezinski, deserve the special attention of statesmen and strategists: a "Zone of Percolating Violence" in Central Eurasia stretching from Turkey to northern India and from Egypt to Kazakstan, characterized by unrest, conflict and violence; and within that zone an area he calls the "Eurasian Balkans," which stretches from southern Russia, eastern Turkey and Iran to Kazakstan, and is characterized   by the aforementioned problems and holds vast untapped energy resources. The "Eurasian Balkans," Brzezinski warns, may be the scene of the next great power rivalry.

Brzezinksi sees the United States as the world's new hegemon and "the first and only truly global power":

> America stands supreme in four decisive domains of global power: militarily, it has an unmatched global reach; economically, it remains the main locomotive of global growth...; technologically, it retains the overall lead in the cutting-edge areas of innovation; and culturally it enjoys an appeal that is unrivaled.

With the collapse of the Soviet Union, the United States became the preponderant power on Eurasia by virtue of its command of the world's seas and oceans and its projected power on the western, southern and eastern regions of the Eurasian landmass. Brzezinski warns, however, that "America's global primacy is directly dependent on how long and how effective its preponderance on the Eurasian continent is sustained."

Students of geopolitics will recognize from the foregoing description of *The Grand Chessboard* that Brzezinski's geopolitical framework has a rich intellectual pedigree. Alexander Hamilton, Thomas Boylston Adams, John Randolph and Thomas Jefferson all had occasion to warn their countrymen to be mindful of the balance of power in Europe. The American naval historian and theorist of seapower, Alfred Thayer Mahan, in his much neglected work, *The Problem of Asia* (1900), foresaw the need for the United States to ally itself with other maritime powers to counter-balance the great landpowers based on Eurasia. (Interestingly, Mahan also described a politically divided and unstable area in Central Asia that he called "the debatable and debated ground," much of which coincides with Brzezinski's concept of the "Eurasian Balkans"). The popular journalist Walter Lippmann, in his masterful book *U.S. Foreign Policy: Shield of the Republic* (1943), recognized that America's security perimeter extended onto the coastlands of Europe and Asia. Yale University's Nicholas Spykman, America's foremost geopolitical theorist and the author of two seminal works, *America's Strategy in World Politics* (1942) and *The Geography of the Peace* (1944), persuasively argued that U.S. security depended on the capability to project power onto the European and Far Eastern sectors of Eurasia—what Spykman called the "Eurasian Rimland." "The safety and independence of this country," wrote Spykman, "can be preserved only by a foreign policy that will make it impossible for the Eurasian landmass to harbor overwhelming dominant power in Europe and the Far East."

Brzezinski's most important intellectual forbearer, however, was the British geographer Sir Halford Mackinder, who has been described, accurately, as the founder of modern geopolitics and "the author of the greatest of all geographical world views." Mackinder's global view is found primarily in two essays, "The Geographical Pivot of History" (1904) and "The Round World and the Winning of the Peace" (1943), and one book, *Democratic Ideals and Reality* (1919). To Mackinder, Eurasia was the "Great Continent," and the potential seat of a world empire. Control of this dominant landmass by a single power or alliance of powers, he warned, would gravely imperil the security of Britain and the United States. This was so, Mackinder explained, because a Eurasian empire which was not distracted by potential continental challengers could use its vast resources to construct overwhelming offensive naval power and achieve command of the seas and oceans that was so vital to the security of Britain and the U.S. Mackinder divided Eurasia into two principal geopolitical regions: the "pivot area" or "heartland" which encompassed roughly the territory of Russia; and the "inner or marginal crescent" or "coastlands" which included Europe, the Middle

East, Southwest Asia, China, Korea and Southeast Asia. The most likely contenders for world empire, according to Mackinder (writing in 1904), were Germany, Russia (or an alliance of the two) and a Sino-Japanese alliance. In 1943, Mackinder recommended and foresaw the emergence of a trans-Atlantic alliance that would prevent the domination of Eurasia by a single power bloc.

What is clear from reading *The Grand Chessboard*, and for that matter Brzezinski's two previous related books—*Game Plan* (1986) and *Out of Control* (1993)—is that Brzezinski's world view is essentially Mackinder's world view updated to account for the events of the last 50 years (Mackinder died in 1947). In fact, in all three books Brzezinski borrows generously from Mackinder's geopolitical concepts and terminology. Mackinder is the giant upon whose shoulders Brzezinski stands.

Interestingly, *Game Plan*, written five years prior to the end of the Cold War, and *The Grand Chessboard*, written six years after the end of the Cold War, present nearly identical global views and identify identical U.S. security interests. That shows that Brzezinski recognizes that America has enduring interests which transcend contemporary events and even major geopolitical changes. The collapse of the Soviet empire did not end history or render geopolitics irrelevant.

That is not to say that Brzezinski in his analysis failed to take into account the impact of recent events on international politics. He recognizes that the most immediate threat to U.S. security interests on Eurasia has vanished, but also that the Soviet collapse created a power vacuum in Central Europe and Central Asia. How that vacuum is filled will likely determine if and when another Eurasian power will challenge America's preponderance on the western region of the great continent. For that reason, Brzezinski is a strong proponent of NATO enlargement, which he views as the most effective mechanism for expanding and consolidating America's preponderance on Eurasia.

Brzezinski also recognizes China's altered status in the post-Cold War world. In *Game Plan*, China was viewed as a *de facto* U.S. ally in preventing Soviet hegemony on Eurasia. In *The Grand Chessboard*, China emerges as the preponderant regional power in the Far East and a rising global power that may attempt to exclude the United States from East Asia. Still, Brzezinski urges American policy-makers to develop a cooperative relationship with China; indeed, he views such a relationship as "imperative for America's Eurasian geostrategy." China, he writes, should become America's "Far East Anchor" in its effort to maintain geopolitical pluralism on Eurasia. He suggests that a failure in this regard could create strains in the U.S.-Japanese-South Korean axis, and could even result in a Sino-Russian alliance or even a Sino-Russian-Iranian alliance against the United States.

One can quibble with some of Brzezinski's judgments and specific policy proposals. He appears to be a little too sanguine about China. Japan and Britain may be more consequential to world politics than he thinks. Neither France nor could even result in a Sino-Russian alliance or even a Sino-Russian-Iranian alliance against the United States.

One can quibble with some of Brzezinski's judgments and specific policy proposals. He appears to be a little too sanguine about China. Japan and Britain may be more consequential to world politics than he thinks. Neither France nor India appear to be "geostrategic players" on the same level as Russia, China and Germany, as Brzezinski suggests. But overall, his analysis of the current world situation and U.S. interests is solidly based on geographical, historical and political realities. Like Mackinder and Spykman before him, Zbigniew Brzezinski focuses our attention on the critical factors of international politics, and provides a much needed geopolitical framework that, if adopted, could discipline what can most generously be called an *ad hoc* approach to international relations by the Clinton administration.

The Sheriff: America's Defense of the New World Order

The daily news stories and commentaries about the war in Iraq and the larger global war against Islamic terrorists usually suffer from a lack of historical and geopolitical perspective. This means that those (probably most) Americans who rely on daily newspapers, television news, talk radio or internet news websites for information about current U.S. foreign policy will be prone to frequent shifts in opinion regarding the wisdom of that policy. For example, symbolic, but essentially meaningless events such as President Bush's landing a plane on an aircraft carrier and the toppling of a statue of Saddam Hussein in Baghdad produced increased support for the war in Iraq, while the plethora of news reports (with accompanying photographs) of the mistreatment of Iraqi prisoners has negatively affected support for the war and has even overshadowed the much less publicized, but much more relevant, facts that U.S. forces have found at least two weapons of mass destruction in Iraq, and there is evidence of links extending over a ten-year time period between Saddam Hussein's regime and al Qaeda terrorists.

In the past, the missing historical and geopolitical perspectives on foreign policy were sometimes supplied in lengthy articles that appeared in foreign policy or opinion journals. Halford Mackinder's "The Round World and the Winning of the Peace" (1943) glimpsed the emerging Cold War world in the midst of the Second World War. George Kennan's "The Sources of Soviet Conduct" (1947) provided intellectual justification for the containment policy in the immediate postwar years. Samuel Huntington's "The Clash of Civilizations" (1993) foresaw the conflict between Islam and the West. Charles Krauthammer's "The Unipolar Moment" (1990) explained the benefits and responsibilities of post-Cold War American hegemony.

In other instances, book-length treatises have appeared at propitious moments to offer guidance to statesmen in their efforts to navigate the ship of state in the troubled waters of global politics. Alfred Thayer Mahan's *The Problem of Asia* (1901) instructed America to extend its security horizons to Europe and Asia. Mackinder's *Democratic Ideals and* Reality (1919) focused attention on the permanent geographical factors that condition world politics. Walter Lippmann's *U.S. Foreign Policy: Shield of the Republic* (1943) and Nicholas Spykman's *America's Strategy in World Politics* (1942) reminded a war-weary America that it must remain engaged in the world after it defeated Naziism. William Bullitt's *The Great Globe Itself* (1946) and James Burnham's *The Struggle for the World* (1947) braced America for its long twilight struggle with the Soviet Union. Hans Morganthau's *Politics Among Nations* (1948) taught that great nations are always engaged in a struggle for power and influence. Henry Kissinger's *Diplomacy* (1994) attempted to reconcile the utopian and realist impulses that influence U.S. foreign policy.

America's assumption of leadership in the global war against international terrorists and the states that support them has led some commentators to refer to the United States as the "American Empire." The British historian Niall Ferguson, among others, advises Americans to accept the imperial burden, while the American political commentator Patrick Buchanan speaks for many when he invokes the sentiments of America's first president to urge a retreat from empire. While the United States' far-flung interests and responsibilities imply an imperial role, Colin Gray, the prolific strategic analyst, is more accurate when he compares America's role in the world to that of a "sheriff" in his latest book, *The Sheriff: America's Defense of the New World Order.*

Gray has been writing about foreign and defense policy since the mid-1970s when he almost single-handedly revived serious scholarly interest in classical geopolitics with his small but brilliant book, *The Geopolitics of the Nuclear Era: Heartland, Rimland and the Technological Revolution.* That book introduced a new generation of students and scholars, including this writer, to the timeless works of Mackinder, Mahan, Spykman and other long-neglected geopolitical theorists. Gray's mind and pen seemed to flow effortlessly after that: *The Future of Land-Based Missile Forces* (1977), *The MX ICBM and National Security* (1981), *Strategic Studies: A Critical Assessment* (1982), *Strategic Studies and Public Policy* (1982), *American Military Space Policy: Information Systems, Weapon Systems and Arms Control* (1984), *Nuclear Strategy and Strategic Planning* (1984), *Nuclear Strategy and National Style* (1986), *Maritime Strategy, Geopolitics and the Defense of the West* (1986), *The Geopolitics of Superpower* (1988), *War, Peace and Victory* (1990), *The Leverage of Sea Power: The Strategic Advantage of Navies in War* (1992), *House of Cards: Why Arms Control Must Fail* (1992), *Weapons Don't Make War: Policy, Strategy and Military Technology* (1993), *The Navy in the Post-Cold War World: The Uses and Value of Strategic Sea Power* (1994), *Military Operations and Maritime Preponderance: Their Relations and Interdependence* (1996), *Explorations in Strategy* (1996), *ICBM and U.S. Strategy* (1999), *Modern Strategy* (1999), *Strategy for Chaos: Revolutions in Military Affairs and the Evidence of History* (2004), and dozens of articles on similar topics.

The Sheriff may be Gray's most important work. It is written at a time when the United States is involved in a dangerous and controversial occupation of Iraq, which the Bush administration views—a view that is hotly disputed—as a central front in the larger war against Islamic terrorism. While Gray's book discusses the war on terror and Iraq, its focus is on the much broader concept of America's role in the world of the twenty-first century.

Gray frames his argument that the United States should act as the world's sheriff as follows: (1) a world order is not self-enforcing, but requires an agent of discipline; (2) the United States is the only potential enforcer of order in today's world; (3) the United States advances its own strategic interests by selectively enforcing the world order; (4) the United States was gradually assuming the role of world sheriff even before the attacks of September 11, 2001; (5) U.S. global preponderance will not last indefinitely, but selecting and implementing the right policies can prolong that preponderance; (6) the role of world sheriff will demand strategies and doctrines that are flexible and adaptable to a variety of international challenges; (7) the world's sheriff needs to develop a grand strategy that will translate military effectiveness into political success; (8) U.S. technological superiority is vital to its role as sheriff, but does not by itself guarantee military and political success; and (9) history is the best guide to understanding what needs to be done, strategically, to succeed as global sheriff.

For nearly forty-five years, from the mid-1940s until the early 1990s, U.S. national security policy focused on the geopolitical imperative of preventing the Soviet Union from dominating the Eurasian landmass. With the collapse of the Soviet Union in 1991, writes Gray, "the country's national security policy was adrift without reliable navigation aids." The Clinton administration, Gray persuasively argues, lacked an "organizing vision" or a "guiding light for high policy" during the 1990s. Instead, for nearly a decade the United States acted in accordance with the "feel-good, heavily multilateralist concepts of global engagement, enlargement...[and] humanitarian interventions." This "strategic pause" of the 1990s, explains Gray, was "brutally terminated by Osama bin Laden and the terrorists of al Qaeda." The September 11 attacks, he writes, required "serious people [to] develop and act on a serious organizing vision for the U.S. role in the world, and for the national security policy and strategy to implement it."

The "serious people" of the George W. Bush administration did precisely that when they released a document in September 2002 entitled *The National Security Strategy*. Most of the news reports and commentaries about that document focused on the brief portions that dealt with the need for preemptive action by the U.S. to forestall potential WMD attacks by terrorists or rogue states. But, as Gray correctly points out, the essence of the new strategy document had its genesis in a 1992 *Defense Planning Guidance* draft written by then Pentagon undersecretary Paul Wolfowitz, who is currently Defense Secretary Donald Rumsfeld's top deputy. The "organizing vision" of both documents is to maintain U.S. global preponderance by preventing the reemergence of a new great power rival and simultaneously preventing a hostile power from dominating regions of the world from which they could threaten U.S. interests.

To be sure, Gray acknowledges the strategic wisdom of preemptive action in some circumstances. He writes:

> To respond after the dread event would be too late. To eschew timely offensive action to disrupt, and hopefully destroy, the WMD threat before it could be launched would be to place a wholly unreasonable burden of perfect performance on active and passive defenses alone. Historical experience, along with the rules of good military practice...argue strongly against conceding the initiative entirely to enemies whose strategic culture has not been molded in graduate seminars at Harvard or Columbia.

But he also recognizes that terrorism and rogue state WMD threats are just some of the problems that the global sheriff will have to deal with during the twenty-first century. "[T]he role of guardian of world order," Gray explains, "carries the duty to oppose and thwart potent threats of disorder from any source, be they state-centric or transnational."

Few Americans want the United States to be the world's policeman. Gray's global sheriff, however, would not be required to police the world. The sheriff would bring its preponderant force to bear only when an event, situation or crisis threatens the world order. Gray points out that the United States performed that role throughout much of the twentieth century by twice intervening in world wars to help thwart bids for global hegemony by Germany, and by anchoring and leading a great coalition to defeat the Soviet Union in the Cold War.

Today, for the time being, the nature of the threat to the world order has changed. There is no great power that currently threatens to upset the global balance of power. Terrorists and rogue states that have or are attempting to acquire WMD, however, pose a clear and present danger to the world order. Recent events in Iraq and the war against al Qaeda show all too clearly that, in Gray's words, if world order is to be enforced, "there is simply no alternative to America as sheriff."

Preventive Containment

The first year-and-a-half of the Clinton Administration has failed to produce a coherent foreign policy or consensus for guiding the nation's external affairs. The Clinton foreign policy team has moved from issue to issue, crisis to crisis, responding to events in a haphazard, makeshift manner. The President himself seems to approach foreign policy issues as unwelcome distractions from his "laser beam"-like focus on domestic concerns.

While the Bush Administration seemed to *manage* foreign policy crises better then Clinton has thus far, the former president also lacked a coherent, systemic approach to world affairs in the wake of the Cold War. The so-called "New World Order," much touted by President Bush, was nothing more than a meaningless, Wilsonian phrase which had no concrete application to the realities of the post-Cold War world.

Bush and Clinton, however, are by no means alone in their inability to formulate or frame a post-containment foreign policy structure. Since the collapse of the Soviet Union the American foreign policy community has been waiting for a new "Mr. X," a successor to George F. Kennan, the State Department's policy planning chief who anonymously theorized and popularized the policy of containment in a brilliant article in the July 1947 issue of *Foreign Affairs*.

Containment, as both a rhetorical and practical policy, had two aspects: the ideological goal of containing the spread of communism, and the geopolitical goal of containing the Soviet Union. Initially, when faced with what appeared to be a monolithic world communist movement headquartered in Moscow, the ideological and geopolitical goals were perceived as being identical. By containing communism we were containing the Soviet empire, and vice-versa.

But as it became increasingly evident that Moscow did not control *all* communist movements and countries, the geopolitical containment of the Soviet empire gained practical, if not rhetorical, ascendancy over containing the spread of communism. In fact, the United States and other Western countries cozied-up to communist regimes in Yugoslavia and Romania that conducted foreign policies independent of Moscow.

Moreover, beginning in the early 1970s we embarked on a *de facto* strategic alliance against the Soviet empire with China, the most populous communist country in the world. Our actions, if not our rhetoric, confirmed that the *key* to containment was geopolitical opposition to the Soviet empire, not ideological opposition to communism.

Viewed in this light, the Cold War was fundamentally a geopolitical struggle wherein the United States and its allies sought to *geographically* contain the Soviet empire. As such, it was not, as some have argued, a *unique* ideological struggle that ended with the demise of Soviet communism. This is not to deny that there was an ideological component to the Cold War, but simply to emphasize that ideological differences only mattered because the Soviet Union posed a serious threat to U.S. security interests.

Far from being a unique episode in world history, the Cold War involved the latest in a series of attempts by great powers to attain hegemony on the Eurasian continent. The NATO alliance, with its strategically complementary U.S.-Japanese alliance and U.S.-Chinese *entente*, was simply the latest in a series of great coalitions formed to oppose hegemonic powers.

To fully appreciate how the Cold War fit within a recurring pattern of geopolitical conflict we must go back over four centuries to the Hapsburg quest for European mastery in the 16th century. At the height of their power, the Hapsburgs ruled Austria, Spain, Burgundy, the Netherlands, the southern half of Italy, Sicily, Sardinia, Bohemia, and Hungary, and held the title of Holy Roman Emperor. The Hapsburg possessions encircled France and threatened the independence of the German princes, the northern Italian states and England. As Paul Kennedy concluded in *The Rise and Fall of the Great Powers*, "had the Hapsburg rulers achieved all of their limited regional aims…the mastery of Europe would virtually have been theirs." Their political ambitions, however, were successfully countered by coalitions of lesser European states formed over a century-and-a-half time period.

The next serious threat to the European balance of power pitted Louis XIV's France against a coalition of powers that included the Netherlands, Austria, Spain, the German states and, eventually, England. In a series of wars between 1689 and 1714, France's hegemonic ambitions were successfully checked and a fragile continental balance of power was preserved.

In the early 19th century, the France of Napoleon Bonaparte achieved European hegemony and threatened Eurasian, perhaps even global, predominance. Had Napoleon either defeated or neutralized Russia, the outcome of France's struggle with Britain might have been different. And as Alexander Hamilton, Thomas Jefferson and John Randolph warned, a France supreme on the Eurasian continent and armed with the British fleet would pose a mortal danger to the United States. Fortunately for the United States and the world, Britain anchored a victorious coalition against France that eventually included Russia, Austria and Prussia. Napoleon was defeated and exiled, and a balance of power was restored on the continent.

In the early to mid-20th century, Germany replaced France as the continental hegemon, while the United States joined and, eventually, replaced Britain as the organizer and financial underwriter of great coalitions opposed to German (and Japanese) ambitions. Thus, the First and Second World Wars of the 20th century in essence repeated the geopolitical struggles of the previous three centuries.

From 1945 until its collapse, the Soviet Union, like Germany, France and the Hapsburgs before it, sought Eurasian hegemony and brought about the formation of a grand coalition of opposing powers anchored by the United States and including the threatened countries in Western Europe, Japan and, ultimately, China. It is in this important respect that the struggle we called the Cold War fits directly within a broad historical process that began over four centuries ago. Less directly, but equally as important, the Cold War fits within the much broader and lengthier historical process of the rise and fall of empires which dates back to the beginning of recorded history.

Is there any reason to conclude that the quest for European, and later Eurasian, mastery which began over four centuries ago has suddenly ended simply because the most recent contender has been defeated? Is there any reason to conclude, further, that human nature and the behavior of nation-states has been so transformed that the quest for power and empire on the part of political leaders and organized political groups has come to a close?

If so, when did this transformation occur? Certainly not in the early part of the 20th century when Imperial Germany's quest for continental domination produced the destruction and brutality of the First World War and spawned modern totalitarian movements. Certainly not in the middle of the 20th century when German and Japanese militarists brought about the Second World War, and Stalin, Hitler and Mao out-performed one another in the art of mass murder.

The latter part of the 20th century likewise contained little evidence that nations and political leaders have forsworn the goals of conquest and hegemony. From Ho Chi Minh to Castro to Idi Amin to Pol Pot to Brezhnev to Saddam Hussein to Slobodan Milosevic, modern political leaders have sought to use the coercive powers of the state to enlarge their personal power and improve the power position of the countries they rule. Modern states have resorted to war, terrorism and even genocide to accomplish their political aims. It is quite probable that we avoided a third world war during the latter part of the 20th century only because of the fears of mutual destruction produced by massive stockpiles of nuclear weapons and delivery systems.

To the 400-year recurring pattern of geopolitical conflict and the unchanging nature of "political man" and nation-states must be added the persistent conditioning factor of geography. The most perceptive observers of international relations, such as Brooks Adams, Fernand Braudel, Alfred Thayer Mahan, Halford Mackinder and Nicholas Spykman, always paid close attention to the impact of geography on world politics. Geographically, the United States is an island off-shore of the Eurasian landmass. That landmass contains the bulk of the world's people and resources and its effective political control by an antagonistic power or alliance of powers would gravely imperil the security and independence of the United States. That is why astute American observers since the founding of our country have recognized that U.S. security is inextricably linked to the balance of power in Europe and Asia. That is why statesmen like John Randolph and Thomas Jefferson were so apprehensive about Napoleon's domination of Europe. And that is why we waged two world wars and one Cold War during the 20th century.

What does all this mean for U.S. post-Cold War strategy? It means that our foreign and defense policies should be geared initially towards *preventing* the emergence of another contender for Eurasian hegemony. It also means, however, that our alliance and defense postures should be such that if and when a potential Eurasian hegemon emerges, we will be well prepared to successfully oppose and *contain* its expansionist ambitions. Such a policy of *preventive containment* is best suited to protect the long-term interests of the United States in the post-Cold War world.

Central and Eastern Europe

Writing in *Foreign Affairs*, Richard Holbrooke, former Assistant Secretary of State for European and Canadian Affairs, advises that "any blueprint for the new security architecture of Europe must focus first on central Europe, the seedbed of more turmoil and tragedy in this century than any other area on the continent." Former National Security Adviser Zbigniew Brzezinski recently commented on the need to eliminate "any potentially disruptive geopolitical vacuum between...Europe and the new Russia." Dominique Moisi and Michael Mertes, foreign policy experts from France and Germany respectively, have urged Western governments to focus on the "security vacuum between Germany and Russia, the area where European wars have historically started." Constantine Menges, professor of international relations at George Washington University, recently urged the governments of central and eastern Europe to "form their own collective security arrangement" to be called the "Central European Defense Organization."

These observers reflect an awareness that for the third time in this century the United States finds itself adrift in a sea of international change in the immediate aftermath of a global conflict. The end of the Cold War has produced a post-war situation which, in its fundamentals, is not unlike the previous post-war situations that emerged from this century's two World Wars. Each post-war situation resulted from the defeat of a power or alliance of powers (Imperial Germany and Austria-Hungary, Nazi Germany and Japan, the Soviet Union) that sought Eurasian hegemony. Each post-war situation witnessed the emergence of a power vacuum in central and eastern Europe. And each post-war situation presented the victorious powers with an opportunity to fill the central-eastern European power vacuum.

In each of the previous two post-war periods in this century, the failure of the victors to adequately settle the central-eastern European question set the stage for the next global conflict. The lesson for our statesmen should be clear: a failure in the present post-war period to eliminate the current central-eastern European power vacuum may set the stage for the next global struggle.

Previous warnings about the pivotal importance of central and eastern Europe, similar to those mentioned above, tragically fell on deaf ears. At the end of the First World War, the brilliant British statesman and geographer, Halford Mackinder, urged the peacemakers at Versailles to turn their attention to central and eastern Europe. "Unless you would lay up trouble for the future," advised Mackinder in his masterful *Democratic Ideals and Reality*, "you cannot now accept any outcome of the war which does not finally dispose of the issue...in East Europe." In words that proved to be all too prophetic, Mackinder warned, "If we accept anything less than a complete solution of the Eastern Question in its largest sense we shall merely have gained a respite, and our descendants will find themselves under the necessity of marshaling their power afresh...." Mackinder's solution was the creation of a "tier of independent states between

Germany and Russia." These newly formed eastern and central European states would be, in Mackinder's description, "the apex of a broad wedge of independence, extending from the Adriatic and Black Seas to the Baltic." To adequately fill the power vacuum created by the First World War, however, this "Middle Tier" of central and eastern European states would require the support of the "outer nations," including Britain and the United States.

The peacemakers at Versailles did create a tier of independent states in the region, but left those states unorganized and unsupported by outside powers. As a result, in the 1930s and early 1940s, Germany and Soviet Russia carved up the region until embarking on their momentous struggle for supremacy. As Mackinder accurately foresaw, the failure by the victors of World War I to organize a sufficient security structure for central and eastern Europe sewed the seeds of the future struggle.

A quarter-century after Mackinder's warning, following the defeat of the Axis powers, the political settlement of central and eastern Europe again dominated the post-war period. Even prior to the war's end, the United States and Britain pressed the Soviets to permit the establishment of freely elected and independent governments in the region, while Stalin, instead, sought to incorporate the region into his empire. Toward the end of the war, British Prime Minister Winston Churchill urged American political and military leaders to push their armies as far east in Europe as possible in order to gain leverage for the coming post-war settlement. As the "iron curtain" descended over central and eastern Europe from the Baltic to the Adriatic Seas, however, the United States, much to Churchill's dismay, began to demobilize its armed forces in Europe and later refrained from using its economic and industrial supremacy and atomic monopoly to force Soviet retrenchment in central and eastern Europe. In the sixth and final volume of his history of the Second World War, aptly entitled *Triumph and Tragedy*, Churchill noted that the American decision to "give up the whole centre and keystone of Europe...seemed to me to be...grave and improvident...." In a letter to President Truman on June 4, 1945, Churchill cautioned, "I view with profound misgivings the retreat of the American Army...in the central sector, thus bringing Soviet power into the heart of Western Europe...." He believed that the territorial division of central and eastern Europe should have been a part of a "general and lasting settlement." Instead, as he lamented in 1948 after the Soviets extended their empire to central and eastern Europe, "we lie in the grip of even worse perils than those we have surmounted."

The tightened Soviet grip on the nations of central and eastern Europe signaled the beginning of the third global conflict of the twentieth century. We have grown accustomed to calling that struggle the "Cold War," but perhaps the American strategist James Burnham was more accurate when in 1944 he referred to it as the "Third World War." Burnham was among the first and one of the few Americans to recognize that Soviet actions in eastern and central Europe, the Middle East and Asia near the war's end were part of a new and different struggle. Our failure towards the end of the war and in its immediate aftermath to contest Soviet domination of central and eastern Europe set the stage for forty-five years of global conflict.

We are now in the midst of the third major post-war period of this century, and once again our focus is, or should be, the political vacuum in central and eastern Europe. But instead of learning from our previous mistakes, instead of rushing in to fill the post-war political vacuum while we have significant advantages (the most significant of which is Russia's internal troubles), we are acting timidly and squandering the opportunity to shape the post-Cold War world. We hesitate to expand NATO to the newly independent nations of central and eastern Europe for fear of offending Russia. We focus more time and effort attempting, with little chance of success, to influence the internal political struggle in Russia, instead of turning our energies toward the more promising endeavor of organizing central and eastern European security structures. We exude timidity, when what is required is boldness and vision tempered by historical perspective.

Taiwan and West Berlin

The steadily increasing political and military pressure being applied by the People's Republic of China against the government and people of the Republic of China on Taiwan has forced the United States to revisit a conflict that spans the second half of the twentieth century. Sooner rather than later, U.S. policymakers will have to decide whether it is in America's interest to defend Taiwan against a military attack by communist China.

Until 1972, the U.S. position was clear: we would defend the Republic of China (ROC) in the event of an attack by the People's Republic of China (PRC), as evidenced by our mutual defense pact with the ROC and by our firm response during the Quemoy and Matsu crisis in the 1950s. From 1972 until the end of the Cold War, the PRC acted as our *de facto* ally in the effort to contain the Soviet Union, even as we formally downgraded, but did not sever, our ties to the ROC. With China as an ally instead of an enemy, the strategic importance of Taiwan declined. The U.S.-Taiwanese relationship, temporarily, was overshadowed by the PRC's role in countering Soviet geopolitical ambitions. When the Cold War ended in 1989-1991, it was only a matter of time before the PRC-ROC conflict re-intensified.

In July 1995, Beijing conducted missile tests near Taiwan. The next month, PRC navy ships and air force planes conducted a joint exercise in the same area. In November 1995, on the eve of ROC legislative elections, the communist Chinese navy conducted blockade and bombing exercises near Dongshan Island, less than 150 miles from Taiwan. In March 1996, obviously timed to coincide with and affect the ROC's presidential election, PRC forces conducted large-scale military exercises in the Taiwan Strait involving surface-to-air missiles, jet fighters, Su-27 interceptors, submarines and short-range ballistic missiles. Douglas Porch, writing in the summer 1999 issue of the *Naval War College Review*, noted that "the joint-force amphibious exercises were the largest observed in the PRC in two decades...," and added that the "planning and execution of the exercises revealed an operational sophistication hitherto unseen in Chinese forces." The United States commendably responded to the PRC's provocation by dispatching two aircraft carrier groups to the region.

PRC diplomatic and military pressure against Taiwan has, nevertheless, continued. On October 15, 1999, Premier Zhu Rongji announced that China would not relinquish the use of force against Taiwan. In June 1999, the PRC agreed to purchase 72 advanced Sukhoi-30 fighter aircraft from Russia. A recent commentary in the *Global Times*, the Communist Party's weekly newspaper in China, warned that China was prepared and ready to attack Taiwan. The PRC's Minister of Defense recently spoke about "punishing" Taiwan for its attempt to "split the motherland." China hinted that it has or is developing a neutron bomb. In November, the *Washington Times* reported that China was expanding its short-range missile base at Yangang, which is located only 275 miles from Taiwan.

The U.S. response has been, at best, mixed. Congress has passed resolutions supporting Taiwan and has urged President Clinton to provide advanced radar (which he agreed to do) and theater missile defenses to the ROC. The position of the Clinton administration, however, is clouded in ambiguity. The State Department has criticized both Taiwan and the PRC, implying that the Taiwanese government, by re-asserting its sovereignty, provoked the Chinese reaction. Worse, as the Heritage Foundation's Harvey J. Feldman recently pointed out, President Clinton departed significantly from the "one China" formula of his predecessors by agreeing to the PRC's "three no's" formula, pledging that the U.S. will not support an independent Taiwan, a "two Chinas" or "one China, one Taiwan" doctrine, or Taiwan's participation in international bodies that require statehood for membership.

The Clinton administration's ambiguity has been harshly criticized by foreign policy experts, including Caspar Weinberger, Richard L. Armitage, Paul Wolfowitz, R. James Woolsey, Jeane J. Kirkpatrick, Elliot Abrams, Richard V. Allen, John R. Bolton, Robert Kagan, Richard Perle, Arthur Waldron, Malcolm Wallop and James Webb. In a joint statement, these experts urged President Clinton and Congress "to make a clear statement of America's commitment to the people of Taiwan." "It has become essential," they wrote:

> that the United States make every effort to deter any form of (mainland) Chinese intimidation of the Republic of China on Taiwan and declare unambiguously that it will come to Taiwan's defense in the event of an attack or a blockade against Taiwan including against the offshore islands of Matsu and Kinmen.

Chinese pressure against Taiwan is reminiscent of soviet attempts to pressure West Berlin into submission in 1948-49, the so-called Berlin blockade. West Berlin was then a tiny island of freedom surrounded by the Soviet-controlled sector of Germany (what became East Germany). Taiwan is an island of freedom offshore the communist-controlled mainland. The Soviets in 1948-49 had geographical and conventional military advantages in the struggle for West Berlin. The Chinese communists have geographical and conventional military advantages in the struggle for Taiwan. The crisis in West Berlin was an early test of how the U.S. would respond to the rising power of Soviet Russia. The crisis in the Taiwan Strait is an early test of how the U.S. will respond to the rising power of the PRC. The defense and survival of West Berlin via the courageous and dramatic airlift of supplies over a 14-month time period proved to the Europeans and the Soviets that the United States had the means and the will to counter Soviet aggression. West Berlin became a symbol of freedom that over time helped to undermine the foundations of Soviet-communist rule in Central and Eastern Europe and in Russia. The defense and survival of a free, democratic Taiwan via U.S. diplomatic and military support would demonstrate to the PRC and the other nations of the Asia-Pacific region that the U.S. has the means and the will to contain Chinese expansion.

Taiwan could become the West Berlin of Asia—the island of freedom that over time helps to undermine communist rule in mainland China.

Taiwan's strategic importance has increased because the PRC is bidding to replace the Soviet Union as the principal challenger to America's global predominance. In the 1950s, when China was our avowed enemy, the great strategic thinker James Burnham wrote in his *National Review* column that Taiwan was "a key link in our western frontier, which runs from the Aleutians down the Japanese Islands, the Ryukyus (Okinowa) and Formosa [Taiwan] to the Philippines." Taiwan's abandonment, wrote Burnham, "would be a staggering disaster for the U.S." Although it is unlikely that the U.S. will purposely "abandon" Taiwan, a continuation of the current ambiguous policy risks a PRC miscalculation that could lead to war or, more likely, a gradual waning of American credibility and influence in the Asia-Pacific region. If the latter occurs, China would be well positioned to replace the U.S. as the region's predominant power. As Burnham once explained: "A great power cannot merely withdraw from a field in which its force has been operating, and leave that field otherwise unchanged, under the play of local influences. The withdrawal of one great power—imperial power, to be more explicit—is inevitably correlated with the advance of a rival power."

The Asian Eclipse of Europe

The age of European-centered geopolitics is over. It lasted, roughly, from the Hapsburg emperor Charles V's bid for global supremacy in the sixteenth century to the fall of the Soviet empire at the end of the twentieth century. For more than four centuries, what happened in Europe affected most of the rest of the world, economically, technologically, culturally, and politically. That is no longer true in the twenty-first century.

Instead, the twenty-first century marks the beginning of the age of Asian-centered geopolitics. What is happening now in Asia — economically, technologically, culturally, demographically, and politically — is affecting most of the rest of the world. American statesmen and policymakers need to accept and understand the consequences of this tectonic shift in global geopolitics.

The great British geographer Sir Halford Mackinder, in his masterful paper "The Geographical Pivot of History" (1904), called the age of European-centered geopolitics "the Columbian epoch." Beginning at the end of the fifteenth century, European explorers discovered and claimed new lands for their countries and, as Mackinder noted, European missionaries, farmers, miners, engineers, and conquerors followed in the explorer's footsteps and "New Europes were created in the... lands discovered."[1] By 1914, as James Burnham pointed out in *Suicide of the West* (1964)[2] and as Niall Ferguson has more recently pointed out in *The War of the World: Twentieth-Century Conflict and the Descent of the West* (2006)[3], European powers (and their offspring, including the United States) dominated the world.

During the four-century time period of European ascendancy, the global geopolitical struggle involved mostly European-based hegemonic powers against coalitions of other mostly European-based powers. Charles V's Spain, Louis XIV's France, Revolutionary France, Napoleon's France, Wilhelmine Germany, Nazi Germany, and the Soviet empire challenged the global balance of power and were countered by mostly European-based coalitions of smaller powers, often funded and led by Great Britain. In the twentieth century, the United States, an offspring of Europe, gradually assumed the geopolitical role of the "holder" of the European balance of power previously played by Great Britain.

George F. Kennan wrote that the First World War was the "seminal catastrophe" of the twentieth century. Old Europe was gone forever. The social constraints of monarchical relations and religion were undermined or seriously weakened. The war unleashed the secular ideological forces of communism and fascism that shaped much of the rest of the century. Hajo Holborn reflected that the First World War initiated, and the Second World War completed, the "political collapse of Europe," meaning the process by which Europe ceased to be a self-contained geopolitical system. The two wars exacted a devastating physical and psychological toll on the old great powers of Western Europe, who recovered physically, but not psychologically. Europe, as Robert Kagan explains at length in his brilliant

Of Paradise and Power: America and Europe in the New World Order, has turned away from power.[4]

Viewed in this light, the Cold War can be seen as the last gasp of a dying European-centered geopolitical system. The countries of Western Europe that, together with Russia, defined the geopolitics of the previous four centuries, played a subsidiary role to the United States during the Cold War. They lost or surrendered their colonial empires, and increasingly became objects of, instead of competitors in, that great global geopolitical struggle. When the Cold War ended, these once great empires became even less significant to global geopolitics. They entered what Kagan calls "a post-historical paradise of peace and relative prosperity," and adopted a "more peaceful strategic culture" that "represents an evolution away from the very different strategic culture that dominated Europe for hundreds of years — at least until World War I."[5]

It will take some time for the United States to fully adapt to this geopolitical change. Since our nation's founding, we have followed, primarily, a Euro-centric national security policy, judging, rightly, that events in Europe would have the greatest impact on our national security. We fought a European power (England), with assistance from other European powers (France and Spain) to gain our independence. President George Washington in his Farewell Address warned his countrymen to avoid involvement in European disputes and conflicts. It was a European power (France) that sold us the Louisiana territory that enabled us to become a continental-sized great power. It was a European power (England) that burned our capital during the War of 1812. President Monroe, in announcing the foreign policy doctrine that bears his name in the early 1820s, cautioned European powers against attempting to colonize territory in the Western Hemisphere. During our Civil War, U.S. policymakers and diplomats worked to discourage European (British and French) intervention on the side of the Confederacy. After the Civil War, we mustered troops to persuade France to surrender its claims to Mexico. At the end of the nineteenth century, we fought a declining European empire (Spain) and, thereby, became a colonial power in Asia and the Pacific.

In the First World War, millions of Americans fought in Europe against the European Central Powers to help restore the global balance of power. In the Second World War, even more millions of Americans fought in Europe and elsewhere against the European Axis Powers of Germany and Italy. (We fought in Asia and the Pacific, too, but defeating our European enemies was deemed more imperative). In the Cold War, we provided economic assistance to war-ravaged Europe (the Marshall Plan), stationed hundreds of thousands of American forces in Europe, signed a mutual security treaty (NATO) with most countries of Western Europe, and pledged to use nuclear weapons to prevent Western Europe from falling to the Soviet empire.

This Euro-centric approach to the world continued even after the end of the Cold War. When the Soviet Union collapsed, instead of re-thinking the need for NATO, we expanded it, even though the security threat that led to NATO's creation had greatly diminished, if not vanished. Indeed, the survival and expansion of NATO is the best evidence that our statesmen and policymakers have not yet fully adjusted to the realities of the twenty-first century's Asian-centered geopolitics.

Those realities are there for all to see. China and India, the two most populous countries in the world, are emerging as Asian great powers, joining Japan and Russia. Russia, China, India, Israel, and Pakistan are nuclear powers, while Iran and North Korea actively seek to join the nuclear club. At the far western end of Asia—the area that we commonly refer to as the Middle East—Islamic fundamentalists and terrorists threaten to undermine the stability of a region that possesses much of the world's energy supplies. At the far eastern end of Asia, the North Korean bid for nuclear weapons and the simmering China-Taiwan dispute threaten to engulf the region in conflict and turmoil.

Thus, since the end of the Cold War, if not before, the former great powers of Europe have willingly withdrawn from the geopolitical rivalry that once dominated their politics and have settled into an era of peaceful coexistence that shows no signs of ending anytime soon. Meanwhile, great power rivalry has shifted to Asia, with much of it located in a broad middle-belt of the continent that Alfred Thayer Mahan, in his 1901 classic *The Problem of Asia*, called "the debatable and debated ground."[6]

Mahan located "the debatable and debated ground" of Asia between 30 and 40 degrees north latitude. This geopolitical region is about six hundred miles in width, and over five thousand miles in length at its broadest point. In Mahan's time, the region had an unsettled political condition and was an object of European great power attention and ambition. Today, this same region contains the rising, populous powers of China and India, four nuclear powers, the main centers of Islamic power, enormous reserves of oil and natural gas in the Middle East and Caspian Sea area, the volatile Korean peninsula, and the offshore power of Japan.

North of this region of Asia lies a diminished but still formidable Russia. To the south, a key maritime highway stretches from the Red Sea through the Arabian Sea and Indian Ocean, through the Bay of Bengal and China Sea, to the Sea of Japan. That maritime highway includes still important chokepoints such as Suez, Aden, the Strait of Hormuz at the entrance to the Persian Gulf, the Strait of Malacca, and the Taiwan Strait.

Unlike in today's Europe, the Asian powers continue to vie with each other for resources and territory, and longstanding disputes (India and Pakistan over Kashmir, the two Koreas over control of the peninsula, China and Taiwan over Taiwan's political status, several Asia-Pacific nations over the Spratly Islands, the countries of the Middle East over land, water, ethnic and religious matters) still fester as they once did among the great powers of Europe.

American policymakers in the early twenty-first century would do well to read the relevant works of Mahan who, in addition to writing on naval history and strategy, wrote voluminously about geopolitics and U.S. foreign policy from 1890 to 1914. Mahan wrote at a time when the United States was emerging as a world power. Throughout most of the nineteenth century, American statesmen had generally followed the broad policy prescriptions of Washington's Farewell Address and the Monroe Doctrine in pursuit of the country's "Manifest Destiny." By avoiding direct involvement in European quarrels, taking advantage of our geographical position in relation to Europe (what George Washington called our "detached and distant situation"), and skillfully exploiting the rivalry among the European great powers to keep them from our shores, the United States by the end of the nineteenth century had grown to a continental giant. But until the aftermath of the Spanish-American War of 1898, it was still mostly an inward looking power.

Beginning eight years before that war, however, Mahan wrote a series of articles in which he advocated a much larger navy, the annexation of the Hawaiian Islands (then known as the Sandwich Islands), strategic cooperation with Great Britain, the building of a canal across the Central American isthmus, and a much broader vision of America's role in the world. The titles of Mahan's articles illuminate his view of America's expanded role in world politics: "The United States Looking Outward," "Preparedness for Naval War," "Hawaii and Our Future Sea Power," "The Possibilities of an Anglo-American Reunion," "A Twentieth Century Outlook." It was time for Americans, Mahan wrote, to cast aside the once prudent counsel of President Washington and assume our proper role as a global power. As he explained in two letters in 1896, "A hundred years ago...[Washington's counsel] was wise and imperative [but] the time has come...when we should and must count for something in the affairs of the world at large."[7]

The Spanish-American War thrust the United States into the Asia-Pacific region. Our capture and conquest of the Philippine Islands and our annexation of Guam, coupled with control of Hawaii meant we now had concrete interests to promote and protect in that part of the world. Mahan understood this new geopolitical fact and it led to the writing of his most profound book on international politics, *The Problem of Asia.*

In Mahan's time, the broad middle-belt of Asia was the object of the European great powers' imperial ambitions. In the twenty-first century, with Europe quiescently enjoying its post-imperial phase of history, the broad middle-belt of Asia is the primary focus of world politics. As Robert D. Kaplan recently pointed out, China's impressive military expansion has lasted for nearly two decades. India may soon possess the third-largest navy in the world. Japan's navy will soon be four times larger than Britain's. Pakistan and South Korea spend a greater percentage of their domestic output on defense than do France and Britain. North Korea is one of the most militarized states on the planet. Kaplan concludes that the "vitality" of the powers in this region "will take us back to an older world of traditional statecraft, in which we will need to tirelessly leverage allies and seek cooperation from competitors."[8] In other words, the powers in the Asia-Pacific region will act like the European powers used to.

In a much longer article on the Hoover Institution's *Policy Review* web site, Tony Corn urges the United States and its NATO allies to recognize and adjust to "the twofold epochal change taking place" in global geopolitics: "the transfer of the center of gravity of the world economy from the Atlantic to the Pacific... and the rise of a 'second nuclear age' in Asia and with it, the concomitant end of three centuries of Western military superiority."

Corn sees the two geopolitical challenges confronting the West in the next thirty years emerging from the Asia-Pacific region. One is the "Long War" against Islamic totalitarianism that is based in the Middle East-Persian Gulf region of West Asia. The other is the "Great Game at Sea" between China and the West for control of the maritime region of Asia that Nicholas Spykman called the "Rimland." Corn recognizes that Europe has at least temporarily stopped thinking geopolitically, but hopes that NATO as a whole, instead of just America, will rise to these challenges. He wants the Atlantic Alliance to "go global" to meet these challenges, but offers little evidence that Europe is ready, let alone able, to follow America's lead in that part of the world.[9]

For the United States, that will mean a more pronounced shift in our strategic focus and our military and economic resources away from Europe and into Asia and the Pacific. Our key strategic allies, instead of Britain, Germany, and France, are now Japan, South Korea, Israel, Turkey, Saudi Arabia, Egypt, Pakistan, Australia, and Taiwan. Continued and greater emphasis should be placed on improving relations with the former Soviet republics of Central Asia, India, Indonesia, Vietnam and the Philippines. Russia, with all its flaws and imperfections, should be viewed as a potential counterweight to China. The U.S. military presence, land and naval forces, should be significantly increased and strengthened in the region—sizeable forces can safely be shifted from Europe to the Asia-Pacific theater.

This does not mean that Europe is unimportant to U.S. security interests. Western Europe remains one of the three key regions of Eurasia that must not be allowed to fall under the control of a power hostile to American interests. But at this moment in history, Western Europe is geopolitically quiet. There are no potential hostile hegemons in Western Europe, nor is there an immediate threat to the independence of Europe by any other Eurasian power. As Lord Palmerston once said, countries have no eternal allies, just eternal interests.

At the end of the First World War, Halford Mackinder observed that "Democracy refuses to think strategically unless and until compelled to do so for purposes of defense." The democrat, he lamented, often thinks in principles, ideals, and morality, instead of reckoning, as he should, with the realities of geography, economics, space and time.[10] The fundamental geopolitical reality of the early twenty-first century is the shift in the global power struggle from Europe to Asia. If the United States is to remain the dominant global power in the twenty-first century, it must adjust its policies to that reality.

ENDNOTES

1. Halford J. Mackinder, "The Geographical Pivot of History," in *Democratic Ideals and Reality* (New York: W.W. Norton & Company, 1962), p. 241, 258.

2. James Burnham, *Suicide of the West: An Essay on the Meaning and Destiny of Liberalism* (Chicago, Il: Regnery Books, 1985).

3. Niall Ferguson, *The War of the World: Twentieth-Century Conflict and the Descent of the West* (New York: The Penguin Press, 2006).

4. Robert Kagan, *Of Paradise and Power: America and Europe in the New World Order* New York: Alfred A. Knopf, 2003).

5. Kagan, *Of Paradise and Power*, pp. 3, 8.

6. Alfred Thayer Mahan, *The Problem of Asia: Its Effect upon International Politics* (New Brunswick, NJ: Transaction Publishers, 2003), with a new introduction by Francis P. Sempa.

7. For an extensive discussion of Mahan's geopolitical writings, see Mahan, *The Problem of Asia*, "Introduction to the Transaction Edition" by Francis P. Sempa at pp. 1-49.

8. Robert D. Kaplan, "Lost at Sea," *New York Times*, www.nytimes.com 2007/09/21/opinion/21kaplan.html

9. Tony Corn, "Perils and Promises of a Global NATO," *Policy Review* (August 2007).

10. Mackinder, *Democratic Ideals and Reality*, pp. 23, 2

Conclusion

Manifest Destiny and the American Empire: Past, Present and Future

As President George W. Bush leaves office, it is not too soon to attempt to place his national security policy in the context of U.S. history. Bush's national security legacy will not become clear for many years, perhaps even decades. President Harry Truman left office in 1953 as a very unpopular and "failed" President. Decades later, when international events confirmed the wisdom of his broad national security policy, Truman was, and is, considered to be a great or near great President.

That is not to say that history will be as kind to Bush as it was to Truman. Truman's broad national security approach, though criticized at the time of his presidency, was generally followed by all of his successors. We do not know whether President Barak Obama or his successors will dramatically change the Bush national security strategy in the next decades, nor do we know whether events will confirm, as they did for Truman, the wisdom of that strategy.

It is appropriate, however, to consider where Bush's broad national security strategy fits in the context of the historic evolution of American national security policy. As is argued below, when viewed from that perspective, Bush's national security strategy is consistent with the expansion of American influence and power that has characterized the evolution of U.S. national security policy. Contrary to popular or conventional opinion, from its Founding to the present, the United States has had imperial ambitions that pushed it to conquer and occupy a continent, acquire overseas possessions, extend its military and diplomatic power to all areas of the globe, and, under Bush, to seek to extend the American system of government to much of the world.

The sociological studies of Vilfredo Pareto, Robert Michels, and James Burnham, among others, have taught us that all countries, regardless of the specific form or type of government, are ruled or governed by elites. Therefore, the national security policies of all countries, including the United States, are the product of elites——statesmen, politicians, writers, thinkers, soldiers, and bureaucrats. In democratic countries, like the United States, the general population often influences and affects national security policies, but only in an indirect way. In studying and analyzing a country's national security policy, it behooves us, then, to focus on the elites who devise, formulate, propose, develop, and implement national security policy.

Of course, not all of a country's elites affect national security policy in the same manner and to the same degree. In the United States under our constitutional structure, the President and his foreign policy advisers have the greatest impact on national security policy. The President commands the armed forces, makes treaties and executive agreements, appoints key national security policymakers, and provides overall direction for the country's foreign policies. The executive branch of government hosts several national security bureaucracies, including the National Security Council staff, the State

Department, the Defense Department, and the Central Intelligence Agency, to name the most prominent.

Congress plays an important role, too, in this area since it controls the purse strings, passes legislation affecting national security policy, approves treaties and many key presidential foreign policy appointments, and investigates and reviews in detail a President's national security policy.

Even the Supreme Court at times has a say in U.S. national security policy when Congress or a President's policies in the area of national security are legally challenged. History shows that more often than not the Court defers to the political branches of government when it comes to national security policymaking, but, as recent Court decisions on President Bush's "war on terror" detention policies demonstrate, the Court sometimes acts to restrain the exercise of executive and/or legislative powers.

Outside the three branches of the federal government, national security elites include reporters and journalists who specialize in national security matters; think-tank scholars and writers who develop and shape ideas on national security matters; and educators who transmit information about national security ideas and policies to future generations of elites.

Other factors help shape a country's national security policy, including, most prominently, geography, demographics, and economics. Those factors, however, affect national security policymaking by their respective impact on a country's elites. They are in essence environmental factors that present both limits and opportunities to elite policymakers.

U.S. national security policy can only be properly understood if it is analyzed in the context of its historical evolution, and that historical evolution begins with its British inheritance.

The elites that first formulated and implemented U.S. national security policy were once colonial elites of the British Empire. Their ideas about governing and conducting national security policy were shaped by their exposure to and involvement in the foreign policies of Great Britain.

Walter Russell Mead in his recent book *God and Gold* brilliantly examines the sources and commonalities of British and American national security policies. Mead traces the origins and successes of what he calls Anglo-American foreign policy to capitalism and sea power. Anglo-American culture nurtured and enabled economic growth and expansion, while Anglo-American geography fostered trade and the development of sea power.

Capitalism and sea power were the twin foundations of the rise and growth of the British Empire from which emerged in 1776 the United States of America. What is commonly referred to as the "American Revolution," is more accurately called the War of Independence. The elites of the new United States were Englishmen or English subjects who fought to separate *politically* from Great Britain, but who nevertheless maintained many British customs, laws, institutions, and traditions.

Among those British traditions that influenced the national security outlook of the new United States were commercial and territorial expansion, i.e. the notion of Empire. The world of the Founding Fathers was a world composed largely of empires—British, French, Russian, Holy Roman, Chinese, etc. Indeed, it would have been strange at that time if the Founding Fathers had not thought in terms of Empire.

Among the Founding Fathers, perhaps no one had a greater impact on shaping early U.S. national security policy than Alexander Hamilton. An illegitimate child born on an island in the Caribbean Sea, Hamilton came to the United States and rose to prominence and power by the sheer force of his intellect and personality. He served as an indispensable military aid to George Washington in the War of Independence, and became Washington's most trusted and influential cabinet member (Treasury Secretary) during his presidency.

Hamilton believed that the United States could develop into a great empire, rivaling, and someday surpassing, in power and influence the empire of Great Britain. As Treasury Secretary, he borrowed from British fiscal policies and practices to promote U.S. trade and commercial expansion, while advocating the construction of a strong U.S. navy.

In 1795, Hamilton described the United States as the "embryo of a great empire." Anticipating the Monroe Doctrine, he envisioned a time when the United States would become "ascendant in the system of American affairs" by "erecting one great American system, superior to the control of all transatlantic force or influence, and able to dictate the terms of the connection between the old and the new world."

Hamilton was an early proponent of what was later called "Manifest Destiny," the idea that the United States should expand territorially from the Atlantic to the Pacific Oceans. In 1798, Hamilton promoted the annexation of all the territory east of the Mississippi River. Despite his intense personal and political animosity towards Thomas Jefferson, he generally applauded the Louisiana Purchase which provided the opportunity for the United States to achieve its "Manifest Destiny."

Hamilton also realized that our ability to achieve a continental empire depended on the European balance of power. For that reason, he promoted the idea of maintaining neutrality between our former enemy Great Britain and our former ally France. President Washington's Neutrality Proclamation of 1793 was based on Washington's and Hamilton's belief that the United States was too weak to involve itself in a great European struggle, and their fear that France, not Great Britain, posed the greatest danger to U.S. security. Hamilton later expressed the fear that the French Empire had "swelled to a gigantic size," aimed at "the control of mankind," and endeavored "to become the Tyrant both of the Sea and Land." Whereas the British Navy, Hamilton wrote, "has repeatedly upheld the balance of power, in opposition to the grasping ambition of France,...[and] has been more than once an effectual shield against real danger."

The national security thinking of Hamilton and Washington culminated in Washington's Farewell Address (1796) which advocated an unsentimental approach to foreign policy based on selfish U.S. national interests, staying-out of wholly European quarrels, and maintaining a "respectable defensive posture" that would enable us to "choose peace or war as our interest, guided by justice, shall counsel." This approach was necessary, according to the Farewell Address, "to gain time [for] our country to settle and mature its yet recent institutions, and to progress without interruption to that degree of strength and consistency, which is necessary to give it...the command of its own fortunes."

The ideas and policies promoted and implemented by Washington and Hamilton planted the seeds of "Manifest Destiny," the Monroe Doctrine, and a recognition that U.S. national security policy must reflect a careful consideration of U.S. interests and the global balance of power.

Ironically, it was Hamilton's political nemesis, Thomas Jefferson, who as President took the greatest practical step toward the fulfillment of the goal of the United States as a continental empire with his controversial purchase from France of the Louisiana Territory in 1803. At a single stroke, as the result of masterful diplomacy by Jefferson with Napoleon's France, the territory of the United States more than doubled in size. Jefferson quickly dispatched a team of explorers to enable the United States to extend political control over the newly purchased land. It was Napoleon who presciently commented about the sale of Louisiana: "They asked of me a city, and I gave them an empire."

Jefferson also wanted to acquire Florida from Spain. In fact, Jefferson envisioned an "Empire of Liberty" that would encompass both the North American and South American continents, "with people speaking the same language, governed in similar forms, and by similar laws."

Jefferson, like Hamilton, also recognized the importance to U.S. national security of a global balance of power. After the British sea triumph at Trafalgar and Napoleon's land victory at Austerlitz, Jefferson commented that, "Our wish ought to be that he who has armies may not have the Dominion of the sea, and that he who has Dominion of the sea may be one who has no armies. In this way we may be quiet; at home at least." Later, in his post-presidential years, Jefferson warned about Napoleon's threat to the global balance of power and the danger it posed to U.S. security.

Jefferson understood, as John Adams and Benjamin Franklin had during the War of Independence, that the United States could reap the benefits of the rivalry among Europe's great powers. Great Britain and France engaged in a century-long struggle for control of North America, so brilliantly analyzed by R.J. Seeley in *The Expansion of England* (1894). Franklin and Adams skillfully exploited the British-French rivalry to gain France's alliance in the War of Independence. Jefferson exploited the same rivalry to persuade Napoleon to sell the Louisiana Territory to the United States. The U.S. defeat of Great Britain in the War of 1812 similarly resulted in part from Britain's continental distractions.

Jefferson's dream of acquiring Florida was realized in 1819, with the Transcontinental Treaty with Spain which resulted from aggressive military moves by General Andrew Jackson and skillful diplomacy by Secretary of State John Quincy Adams.

Secretary of State Adams also realized that Manifest Destiny could not be achieved if the European great powers continued to colonize in the Western Hemisphere. This apprehension led Adams and his boss, President James Monroe, to formulate and announce the Monroe Doctrine (1823) which warned the European powers that the United States would resist their efforts to acquire new colonies in the Western Hemisphere. The Monroe Doctrine nicely complemented Washington's Farewell Address, and both supported the idea of Manifest Destiny. The Farewell Address said that the U.S. would refrain from intervening in European conflicts. The Monroe Doctrine was designed to prevent European interference in the Americas. This approach to national security policy would enable the United States to concentrate on completing its conquest, occupation and political appropriation of the continent.

The Farewell Address guided U.S. national security policy throughout most of the nineteenth century. The Monroe Doctrine continues to guide U.S. national security policy into the twenty-first century.

Jefferson's "Empire of Liberty," however, did not mean liberty for the Native Americans that inhabited some of the lands acquired by the United States. Instead, using a combination of trickery, diplomacy and coercion, the United States gradually removed all Native American obstacles to westward expansion. This "Indian removal" policy continued until the end of the nineteenth century. "Manifest Destiny" at times was achieved at a heavy moral price.

The next frontier of Manifest Destiny was the southwestern portion of the continent that bordered Mexico. In the 1830s and 1840s, Americans migrated and settled in the area of Texas which briefly became an independent republic and subsequently was annexed to the United States as a result of its victory in the Mexican War (1846-48). The huge swath of territory acquired by the United States as a result of President Polk's war virtually completed America's continental empire. Polk ranks with Jefferson as the most expansionist Presidents in U.S. history. They are, in large part, the architects of Manifest Destiny.

If Jefferson and Polk are the two main architects of Manifest Destiny, Lincoln is the savior of Manifest Destiny. As the United States geographically expanded, so too did the divisive political and moral issue of slavery. Previous compromises had delayed, but not resolved the conflict over slavery and states versus federal power, and Lincoln's election in 1860 brought compromise to an end. The result was the most destructive conflict in U.S. history——the American Civil War——which claimed the lives of more than 600,000 Americans.

The outcome of the Civil War determined whether the geographic space in the center of the North American continent would be occupied buy one or two countries. Had Lincoln and the Union not achieved victory, Manifest Destiny would have been stopped dead in its tracks and the subsequent history of the world would have been very different. For instance, would a much smaller United States faced with a powerful southern neighbor below the Mason-Dixon Line have been able to intervene in Spain's conflict with Cuban rebels in 1898; or have been able to intervene to tip the balance in the Allies favor in the First

World War; or to intervene on a global scale to defeat the Axis powers in the Second World War; or to anchor a global coalition to contain the Soviet Union in the Cold War?

Great Britain and France clearly understood what was at stake in the American Civil War, and both powers threatened to intervene on the side of the Confederacy in an effort to limit and restrict the growth of American power. During the war, Russia's minister to Great Britain reported that, "the English Government...desires the separation of North America into two republics, which will watch each other jealously and counterbalance each other. Then England, on terms of peace and commerce with both, would have nothing to fear from either; for she would dominate them, restraining them by their rival ambitions." In September 1861, former Colonial Secretary Edward Bulwar-Lytton remarked that a permanent division of the United States would benefit the "safety of Europe." A continental-sized United States, he explained, "hung over Europe like a gathering and destructive thundercloud...[but] as America shall become subdivided into separate states...her ambition would be less formidable for the rest of the world." France's minister to Washington, Edouard-Henri Mercier, was among the strongest advocates of European intervention in support of the Confederacy.

The Union victory, however, meant that Manifest Destiny would continue, and the United States would dominate North America and the Western Hemisphere.

The Spanish-American War of 1898 effectively extended U.S. political control to overseas territories. Having consolidated political control of the center of North America, and with relatively weak neighbors to the north (Canada) and south (Mexico), the original goal of Manifest Destiny was complete. Even before the Spanish-American War, however, there were voices in the United States urging the country and its leaders to play a larger role on the world stage.

In 1890, an unknown naval captain working at the Naval War College in Newport, Rhode Island, authored a book entitled *The Influence of Sea Power upon History 1660-1783*, which analyzed the role of the British Navy in helping to construct and maintain the world's greatest empire. The captain, Alfred Thayer Mahan, was soon known throughout the world. His book was published in most of the world's major languages and was studied by the navies of the great powers. It is said that Kaiser Wilhelm II ordered every German warship to have a copy of Mahan's book on board.

Mahan wrote not only about the history of sea power, but also authored books and articles on naval strategy and international politics. He became the leading intellectual proponent of American overseas expansion, and he corresponded with and became an informal adviser to President Theodore Roosevelt.

Roosevelt shared Mahan's vision of the United States as a great naval power and as the geopolitical successor to the British Empire. This meant the establishment and maintenance of an overseas empire and greater participation in the global balance of power.

The Spanish-American War presented the opportunity for the United States to assume a greater role in world affairs, and it did so by annexing Hawaii, the

Philippine Islands, Guam, and Puerto Rico, and ending Spain's control of Cuba. When Roosevelt became President after the assassination of William McKinley in 1901, the United States strengthened its navy, forcibly crushed a Philippine rebellion, began construction of an inter-oceanic canal across the isthmus of Panama, negotiated an end to the Russo-Japanese War, and sent the navy on a world tour to demonstrate America's emergence as a global power.

It was also during Roosevelt's administration that Secretary of State John Hay extended U.S. influence into Asia via the "Open Door" policy. The United States was now an Atlantic and a Pacific power with interests in Europe and Asia. The oceans were no longer seen as defensive barriers protecting America from the great power conflicts of the Old World. Increasingly evident to Mahan, Roosevelt and others was that America's first lines of defense were the shores of Europe and Asia from which a great power could launch an attack against us.

Just as the United States was emerging onto the world stage, Europe lurched toward the catastrophe of the First World War. The tradition of Washington's Farewell Address counseled against involvement in Europe's Great War, and for three years, despite loud protests from Theodore Roosevelt and others, President Woodrow Wilson maintained American neutrality. Germany's policy of unrestricted submarine warfare and its secret efforts to induce Mexico to ally with it against the United States (the Zimmerman Telegram), however, forced Wilson to recognize the threat to U.S. security posed by a hostile European hegemon. U.S. forces fighting on European soil in 1917-18 tipped the balance against the Central Powers. Germany surrendered. Wilson's subsequent attempt to impose a high-minded peace upon the world, however, failed. The United States remained aloof from the European balance of power throughout the 1920s and 1930s.

But, as the events of the next twenty-five years would demonstrate, the world had changed. The European world order collapsed on the battlefields of France. The United States could no longer afford the luxury of remaining aloof from the global balance of power. As Mahan had foreseen, the United States had become the geopolitical successor to the British Empire.

It took Nazi Germany's conquest of most of Europe in the 1930s and early 1940s and Japan's attack on Pearl Harbor in December 1941 for most Americans to realize that their security was intimately connected to the global balance of power. President Franklin Roosevelt recognized this earlier than most Americans, but he hesitated to get too far ahead of American opinion. When the country went to war, however, FDR waged war with the idea that the United States would play a major role in constructing the postwar order.

The reach of American power in the Second World War was truly remarkable. It fought on virtually every continent, and its navy dominated the oceans and seas at the end of the war. It out-produced every other major power in war material. By the war's end, the U.S. had 12 million men under arms, it had command of the world's oceans, it was the only great power that suffered relatively little damage to its homeland, and it was the world's only atomic power.

During the war, Yale University's Nicholas Spykman, in *America's Strategy in World Politics* (1942) and *The Geography of the Peace* (1944), urged the United States to remain an active participant in the European and Asian balances of power. The popular American journalist Walter Lippmann issued similar advice in his influential book, *U.S. Foreign Policy: Shield of the Republic* (1943). Despite the popular sentiment to "bring the boys home" after the war, an increasing number of American elites recognized that the United States, for its own security, needed to play a major role in shaping the postwar world order.

At the wartime summits, FDR, Churchill and Stalin negotiated and planned the postwar order. Like Wilson before him, FDR placed great hopes in a world organization to maintain the postwar peace; and like Wilson, FDR misjudged the fundamental nature of international relations. But FDR did recognize and accept the idea that the United States would supplant the British Empire as the anchor of the postwar economic and geopolitical world order. U.S.-led international political and economic institutions would help to shape the postwar order. Manifest Destiny was in some respects now global in nature.

The postwar threat posed by the Soviet Union resulted in the United States assuming even greater imperial burdens. Great Britain's decline created a geopolitical power vacuum that was gradually filled by the United States. A then largely unknown U.S. diplomat named George F. Kennan in a "Long Telegram" written from Moscow in 1946 and a seminal article in *Foreign Affairs* entitled "The Sources of Soviet Conduct" in 1947, analyzed the Soviet geopolitical threat and urged a policy of "firm and vigilant containment" of Soviet expansionist tendencies.

Containment manifested itself in several ways. The Truman Doctrine extended U.S. aid to Greece and Turkey. The Marshall Plan provided massive economic assistance to Western Europe. The creation of NATO extended a U.S. security guarantee to most of Western Europe and resulted in stationing U.S. military forces in Europe. The Korean War, the U.S.-Japanese defense pact, and a mutual defense pact with Taiwan extended U.S. security guarantees to key Asian and Pacific powers. U.S. military forces were stationed in Japan, Korea, and key bases in the Philippines. The French retreat from Southeast Asia led to U.S. commitments to South Vietnam.

Most of these unprecedented global security commitments by the United States—a sort of global "Manifest Destiny"—were explained and justified in a remarkable document known as NSC-68. Written in 1950 by a team of national security experts headed by Paul Nitze, then director of the State Department's policy planning staff, and only unclassified in the mid 1970s, NSC-68 was the blueprint for implementing the policy of containment. It explained the nature of the Soviet threat to the U.S. and the West and outlined a massive military and political response to that threat.

The national security policies of every U.S. President during the Cold War reflected the broad strategy set forth in NSC-68. The U.S. nuclear arms build-up and Cold War alliances; U.S. participation in the Vietnam War; U.S. policies in the Middle East; the strategic exploitation of the Sino-Soviet rift; and the exploitation of the economic and political vulnerabilities of the Soviet Empire in the 1980s have their genesis in NSC-68.

During a 43-year time period, the United States under eight Presidents constructed and anchored a global coalition of powers, including the NATO countries, Japan, the Philippines, South Korea, several countries in the Middle East-Persian Gulf region, and China, that effectively contained the Soviet Union until the Soviet system collapsed in 1989-91. In historical perspective, it was reminiscent of the coalitions constructed and anchored by Great Britain to defeat France under Louis XIV in the seventeenth and early eighteenth centuries and Napoleon Bonaparte in the late eighteenth and early nineteenth centuries.

The collapse of the Soviet Empire produced a situation where the United States was the lone global superpower. Some analysts compared the U.S. geopolitical situation to the Roman Empire at the height of its power. Charles Krauthammer described it as the "unipolar moment," recognizing the unmatched U.S. global influence and power, but also recognizing it as a temporary and perhaps very brief ("moment") situation.

The George H.W. Bush administration spoke about a "new world order," but soon found itself at war in the Persian Gulf with an Iraqi regime that still operated by the "old" rules. After a swift victory in the Gulf War, Bush security officials looked to frame a national security policy that would prevent the rise of a new "peer competitor" to the United States.

The Clinton administration, like its predecessor, sought to take advantage of the unipolar moment by politically and economically engaging potential peer competitors, such as China, while focusing on trade, economics, and multilateral solutions to global problems. Clinton lacked an easily identifiable enemy at which to focus a national security strategy, but intervened in Somalia, Haiti, and the Balkans on little more than humanitarian grounds. Clinton, like his predecessor, continued to expand NATO to include several former East bloc countries, and continued efforts to enforce Iraqi compliance with UN resolutions imposed after the Gulf War. It also dealt in a less than comprehensive manner with attacks on U.S. interests by Islamic terrorists.

President George W. Bush entered office in January 2001 with every intention of scaling-back U.S. efforts at nation-building and humanitarian intervention. The terror attacks on September 11, 2001 changed all that. Bush responded with an ambitious national security strategy that sought to defeat our immediate terrorist enemies, change or remove "rogue" regimes that provide support to terrorists and have access to weapons of mass destruction and who refuse to end their support of terrorism, and to democratize the Middle East so that it will no longer serve as a breeding ground for Islamic terrorists.

In practical terms, Bush attacked the Taliban regime in Afghanistan which hosted and supported international terrorists, including Al Qaeda, and invaded Iraq to remove the threat of a regime that had previously possessed and used weapons of mass destruction, had ties to terrorist groups, and which had failed to comply with numerous UN resolutions imposed after the first Gulf War. Both the Taliban in Afghanistan and Saddam Hussein's regime in Iraq fell quickly to

U.S. and allied military power, but in both countries insurgents upset U.S. plans for postwar political reconstruction.

George W. Bush's national security strategy, although attacked by realists as being too ambitious and utopian, is consistent with the evolution of the American Empire. In our country's first century, under the goal of Manifest Destiny, we sought to shape the political order of North America and the Western Hemisphere, and largely succeeded. In the country's second century, we emerged onto the global stage and gradually assumed the geopolitical role of Great Britain by establishing and maintaining a world order in the face of challenges by revolutionary totalitarian powers. In the current century, the Bush national security policy sought to extend the American system of government to other parts of the globe in an effort to change or remove dangerous rogue states and regimes that succor, support and breed international *jihadists*. Bush's national security strategy was simply another, much broader, version of Manifest Destiny.

During the recent presidential campaign, Barak Obama was critical of Bush's Iraq policy, but supportive of the broader "war on terror," even promising to send *more* U.S. forces to Afghanistan and, in certain circumstances, launch military strikes into Pakistan in an effort to defeat our terrorist enemies. President Obama may very well pursue some, if not all, aspects of the Bush strategy. It is as yet unclear whether Obama will, like Bush, seek to democratize the Middle East and confront rogue states who have access to weapons of mass destruction and provide assistance to international terrorists. If Obama does generally follow the Bush strategy, and his policies succeed or are successful under his successors, history may be much kinder to Bush than most people now believe. As Edward N. Luttwak has pointed out, if the broad Bush national security strategy ultimately prevails in the war against Islamic *jihadism*, Iraq will be considered a costly sideshow in an otherwise successful policy; just as the domestically divisive Korean and Vietnam Wars were considered costly sideshows in the overall successful policy of containment.

About the Author

Francis P. Sempa is the author of *Geopolitics: From the Cold War to the 21ˢᵗ Century*, and has written introductions to four books on U.S. foreign policy. He has authored numerous articles, essays, and reviews for such publications as *Strategic Review*, *American Diplomacy*, *Presidential Studies Quarterly*, *The National Interest*, the *Washington Times*, *National Review*, the *Human Rights Review*, and the *International Social Science Review*. He is a contributor to the 1990 volume, *The Conduct of American Foreign Policy Debated*. He is an Assistant United States Attorney for the Middle District of Pennsylvania, an adjunct professor of political science at Wilkes University, and a contributing editor to *American Diplomacy*.

Index